MEDITATIONS ON
HOLINESS

THOMAS D. LOGIE

Order this book online at www.trafford.com
or email orders@trafford.com

Most Trafford titles are also available at major online book retailers.

Printed in the United States of America.

ISBN: 978-1-4907-2928-2 (sc)
ISBN: 978-1-4907-2927-5 (e)

Trafford rev. 02/27/2014

www.trafford.com
North America & international
toll-free: 1 888 232 4444 (USA & Canada)
fax: 812 355 4082

CONTENTS

Chapter 1 An Introduction to Holiness 1

Chapter 2 Holiness, Vigilance & Prayer 20

Chapter 3 Holy and Polluted Love 24

Chapter 4 Holiness at Home as a Foundation of Ministry 35

Chapter 5 Holiness, Work & Economic Impact 38

    Trends Unfavorable To Christians In Work: 43

    Technological Trends Reducing Employment
        Affecting Christian And Non-Christian Alike 44

Chapter 6 Acrostic of Jesus Christ Pertaining to Holiness: 47

Chapter 7 Sermons and Meditations on Holiness, Fire & Love 63

    Fair Warning! 63

    Holiness: Standing With God Even If It Means
        Standing Alone On Earth 68

    Holiness In The Face Of Opposition 71

    Holiness: The Depth Of Conversion 73

    Holiness: Countdown 74

    Holiness Or Hell? 78

    Holiness: Approval, Discipline, Or Both? 82

    Holiness & Anger 84

    Benefits Of Holiness While We Await Heaven 86

    Holiness & Humility Go Together Like Vanilla Ice
        Cream And Chocolate Sauce 89

Holiness: The Example Of David's Life (Part 1)................. 91

Holiness—The Example Of David's Life (Part 2)............... 96

Holiness Means Being People Of The Holy Scriptures..... 102

Holiness Of Thought And Speech.................................... 105

Benefits Of A Holy Reputation In Heaven....................... 108

Holiness & Hope.. 111

A HOLY REPUTATION: AN ILLUSTRATION FROM NATURE

Revelation 19:8 speaks of the Bride of Christ in terms of her holiness in the eyes of Jesus Christ, the Bridegroom. The Bible says, *"And to her it was granted to be clothed in fine linen, clean and white, for the fine linen is the righteousness of saints."* In my mind it is possible to understand "righteousness" first of all as the righteousness given to the Bride by Jesus Christ through His death, burial and resurrection, and secondarily her righteous character and actions rooted in the righteousness that He has given her. In this photograph is a reminder in nature of the future white linen of the Bride, although nothing white in our current world will match the dazzling white and purity of the sinless universe to come. Even more, nothing white in the current creation will match the purity of the Lord Jesus Christ as reflected in Revelation 1:14 and like passages.

HOLINESS & HUMILITY: AN ILLUSTRATION FROM NATURE

"But I am a worm and no man, a reproach of men and despised by the people." Psalm 22:6, referring to Jesus Christ. *"Look even at the moon, that it does not shine; yes, the stars are not pure in His sight. How much less man, a worm? And the Son of Man, a worm?"* Job 25:5-6.

How far down did the humility of the Lord Jesus go? While this bird has a fish instead of a worm, the picture should give us a visual clue. The fish is helpless, just as the Lord Jesus was on the Cross. If not dead yet in the picture, the fish is about to die and is as good as dead. So the Lord Jesus humbled Himself to die at the hands of wicked people. The Holy One shows us true humility.

But this picture does not show the finish. The Lord Jesus rose from the dead. Because He humbled Himself all the way to a criminal's tortuous death on the Cross, *"God also has highly exalted Him and given Him a name which is above every name, that at the name of Jesus every knee shall bow . . . and every tongue confess that Jesus Christ is Lord, to the glory of God the Father.* Philippians 2:9-11. While we will never reach the height of the Lord Jesus, the same principle applies to us: *"Humble yourselves in the sight of the Lord, and He will lift you up."* James 4:10.

CHAPTER 1

---◦◦◦---

An Introduction to Holiness

Holiness. Sanctification. They sound like foreign words to many modern readers. Holiness has its word origin in Greek; sanctification comes from Latin. Both of them have the same basic meaning: <u>set apart from sin and set apart to God.</u> In modern Western culture, the very idea of being "set apart" is scary. We are being conditioned to follow one another because "everybody does it." Being socially isolated is to be avoided like the plague. This is not totally new. Daniel's three friends in Daniel 3 stood out in contrast to the crowd when they defied King Nebuchadnezzar's order to bow down to the golden image. Jeremiah had few friends in high places when he counseled a succession of kings to submit to King Nebuchadnezzar because God said so. He was right but nearly alone. For a short time he was thrown into a muddy well bottom. Elijah was alone as the prophet of God on top of Mount Carmel, against 850 prophets of the false god Baal. When he was imprisoned for the last time before his execution, Paul had only Luke, his physician, with him. And Jesus Christ alone bore our sins on the Cross, although John and some women were nearby.

These examples are sufficient to tell us that even in the days of the Bible that holiness often had heavy costs in terms of human companionship. Other Scriptures sound the same note:

> *Everyone that has forsaken houses, or brothers or sisters, or father or mother or children or wife, or lands, for My name's sake, shall receive one hundredfold, and inherit everlasting life.* Matthew 19:29 (spoken by the Lord Jesus)

Whosoever therefore will be the friend of the world is the enemy of God. James 4:4

They think it strange that you do not run with them to the same excess of riot, speaking evil of you. 1 Peter 4:4.

Evil companions corrupt good morals. 1 Corinthians 15:33.

To be holy, one must be willing to stand apart and in some cases even to stand alone or nearly alone. Think about Lot, who lived in Sodom and was trying to raise a family for God. He did not enjoy it. If one looks back at Genesis 19, Lot's neighbors went so far as to try to invade his home in order to seize and violate sexually his visitors, not realizing that his visitors were actually avenging angels. Before that terrible night, Lot was *"vexed with the filthy behavior of the wicked. For that righteous man dwelling among them in seeing and hearing, vexed his righteous soul from day to day with their unlawful deeds."* 2 Peter 2:7-8. Lot lost not only his wealth, but also his home and his wife as judgment fell on Sodom and the surrounding region. But he did not lose his soul. Today's Christians or future generations may have to endure similar hatred and trials before we are vindicated and rewarded at the Last Judgment.

The Apostle Paul in 1 Corinthians 7:29-30 probably had in mind persecution during his own lifetime which led to Paul's own execution, *"The time is short. It remains that those who have wives shall be as though they had none; and those that weep as though they did not weep; and those that rejoice as though they did not rejoice, and those that buy as though they did not possess."* Paul, the unmarried apostle, and Peter, the married apostle, were executed close in time to each other. But these words will apply equally well to Christians under persecution in any era and to the Christians living near the Last Days. Our Lord Jesus said, *"If they have persecuted Me they will also persecute you."* (John 15:20) So once more we have to face the probability that most of humanity will declare themselves to be our enemies and behave accordingly, especially as the return of the Lord Jesus draws closer.

Like being set apart, self-denial is an alien concept in modern Western culture. The world encourages self-expression virtually without qualification, even to the point of suicide to express one's despair or various form of sexual self-gratification outside of marriage to express one's inner lack of self-control. Lest you think that I exaggerate, consider the extent to which physician-assisted suicide is now practiced in Belgium. This concept of "honorable suicide" sounds like the voluntary suicide expected of a losing German general such as Model or of a person such as Cleopatra who considered herself a failure in the ancient world. However, it would not include compelled suicides such as those of Socrates or Rommel. There are some thoughts such as despair that we may have that should be prayed to God only and never expressed to any other human being on earth.

Why is self-denial necessary for holiness? Consider that Ephesians 2 tells us that we are born physically alive but spiritually dead. If we express our dead spirits, we are emitting figurative odors of a corpse. As Paul wrote of unsaved people in Romans 3:13: *"Their throat is an open tomb . . ."* While self-denial is not enough, it is an essential early step in a total process to start our new life as a sweet-smelling savor to God by stopping the natural moral stench. On top of self-denial must come the expression of the character of the Lord Jesus Christ. Matthew 12:43-45 is a warning about temporary outward reformation without the inward presence of the Holy Spirit. That surface reformation and temporary self-denial leaves a void that will become worse than the original state later on. For salvation and for holiness, that void must be filled by the Holy Spirit, Who is the only permanent solution. For an analogy, envision the necessary removal of the inflamed pulp of a severely infected tooth in order to quell the pain. One cannot leave the interior empty; it must be packed in a sterile manner. So the dead, putrefying space in our soul must be cleansed and filled with the Holy Spirit. The difference from the tooth example is that the Holy Spirit is living whereas the tooth packing is dead. So the filling of the Spirit not only quells infection but gives life.

This is part of what the Lord Jesus meant as He spoke in Mark 8:34: *"Whosoever will come after Me, let him deny himself and take up his cross and follow Me."*

Although the Parable of the Sower in Matthew 13 does not mention the Holy Spirit, it does show that 3 of the 4 types of soil produce foliage in response to the Word of God. But only one of the soil types produces a good crop. For different reasons, the other two soils do not produce a stable root system and therefore die out without a crop. And both Matthew 7 and John 15 teach the necessity of good fruit as evidence of genuine salvation. While the metaphors are different, these Scriptures are united in teaching that true holiness produces lasting results, including lasting changes of character and lifestyle. The Holy Spirit is of course stable and will when necessary fracture the rocky parts of our hearts and minds to remove sin and to make room for the teachings and character of Jesus Christ. *"Do not let sin therefore reign in your mortal body that you should obey it with its lusts, nor yield your members as instruments of unrighteousness to sin, but yield yourselves to God as those who are alive from the dead, and your members as instruments of righteousness to God."* Romans 6:12-13. So God, not our self-will, is to be in control of our body.

For the short run, it is so much easier to conform to the world. But our time on earth is a mere blink compared to our conscious eternity. We are confronted with the command of the Holy Spirit in Hebrews 12:14, *"Follow peace with all, and holiness, without which no man shall see the Lord."* It is necessary to pursue peace with our neighbors because it will not come naturally. But we must also pursue holiness. There is a tension between the two, because the ways of holiness lead us away from the impulses of most men and women. But holiness is so important that we will not see the Lord Jesus without it. It is not that we earn salvation, but rather that holiness is the necessary evidence of salvation just as a passport is a necessary document to identify one's country of citizenship or a boarding pass is a necessary evidence of one's right to enter an airplane. *"For our citizenship is in heaven, from where we also look for the Savior, the Lord Jesus Christ."* Philippians 3:20. Viewed from this perspective, we are foreigners on earth with our permanent home in heaven. Once more we can see how we are separated from the majority of humanity.

The Apostle Paul tells us that we are "ambassadors" for Christ in 2 Corinthians 5:20. Nobody sends an ambassador to one's own country. Rather, an ambassador represents his or her country to a foreign land, faithfully transmitting the message of his or her government. Even though we were born on earth, with our new birth from above we now are citizens of heaven notwithstanding our temporary location on earth.

While our presentation must be framed in a way that our hearers on earth can comprehend and receive, the substance of our message is controlled by Jesus Christ, our Lord and King. We must anticipate disagreements and in many cases even hatred because of the substance of our message. Jeremiah hardly made the Best Seller list of King Jehoiakim, who caused his first scroll of warning to be burned. Daniel was thrown into a den full of lions because of jealousy from his co-workers. Both of these prophets survived their initial brushes with death, but Isaiah was sawed in half by King Manasseh, and he was not the only prophet to die for his faith. So being an ambassador can be dangerous. Christ's ambassadors are not always afforded diplomatic immunity. But the fact that we are viewed as ambassadors emphasizes our separation from this world and our former ways of life.

Some people think that they should try to serve God in isolation from everyone or at least in isolation from the workaday world. Rarely is this right. Most human beings need companionship as well as some time of isolation to think and pray. Among adults, part of this companionship is usually in marriage between husband and wife. The Apostle Paul, though unmarried, normally took care not to be completely alone in his missionaries journeys, although unexpected events did cause him to be alone temporarily in Athens. But Paul himself makes it clear that his state of singleness was the exception, not the rule.

Walter Hilton was a Christian scholar in England during the time of Wycliffe, toward the end of the 1300s. When a leader in the community asked Hilton after his salvation from sin whether he should enter a monastery, Hilton advised against that in favor of what he called a "mixed life." This concept was that the convert should live for God as he carried out his responsibilities, which included being a landlord, magistrate and military officer. Modernizing this concept, the "mixed life" includes both direct worship of God and service to God through human duties which vary with each individual. S. Truett Cathay (Chick Fil-A), the original J.C. Penney and William Colgate are American examples of this "mixed life." In his later years J.P. Morgan was another example. So was Theodore Roosevelt. These responsibilities may include political and military service, taking one's place in one's family, investment, education, work and charitable activities, among other things. Hilton did not advocate for most Christians that they isolate themselves in a monastery or in church. A keynote of his "mixed life" is taking Christ and the Bible into everyday life of the community. Hilton believed that pastors also should live in their community of service. As the Apostle Paul put it, we are to *"shine as lights in the world."* Philippians 2:15. When the Corinthians misunderstood some advice from Paul about withdrawing from evildoers, Paul corrected them by pointing out that if they were to withdraw from evildoers generally, *"you would need to go out of the world."* 1 Corinthians 5:10. Paul's instructions were confined to withdrawing from particular evildoers who claimed the name of Jesus Christ. I would infer that using the name of Jesus Christ as a cover for evil was especially odious to Paul. For a more complete excerpt on Hilton's idea of the "mixed life," look at The Law of Love, edited by David Lyle Jeffrey, Walter E. Eerdmans Publishing Company, 1988, pp. 229-235. For our purposes the main idea is that the Christian life is lived in contact with the world even though as Christians we are fundamentally unlike the world and are becoming more like God instead.

If one reads Romans 3:9-20, one will find a comprehensive indictment by God against humanity. In Romans 1:16 and the following verses, one can find a Bill of Particulars naming specific acts and attitudes that support the indictment. The sweeping reach of both the indictment and of the Bill of Particulars shows the yawning gap between God and the mass of humanity. So to side with God and agree that His charges are valid involves a separation from the attitudes and actions of the majority. For a historical example, contrast during the Nuremberg Nazi trials the attitude of Albert Speer (who thought the trial was necessary and many of the charges just) with the defiant attitudes of the majority of the defendants led by Goering. Naturally, Speer was ostracized by many of the other defendants. The Apostle Paul observed in 1 Corinthians 4:13 that *"we are made as the filth of the world, the offscouring of all things to this day."* Or as the Lord Jesus taught, *"wide is the gate and broad is the way that leads to destruction, and there are many who go by that route. Because strait is the gate and narrow is the way that leads to life, and there are few that find it."* Matthew 7:13-14.

So is the Christian life a lonely life? In terms of flesh-and-blood companionship, it often is, although some of the strongest marriages, families and friendships in all of history have been between and among Christians. But there is a priceless benefit to separation to God whether or not one is married: fellowship with the eternal God Himself. Abraham as the "father of the faithful" (Romans 4:1,12; Galatians 3:7) had a fellowship with God so close that God forewarned Abraham of the destruction of Sodom (Genesis 18:16-22). Earlier (Genesis 15) God had made a covenant with Abraham involving a personal appearance of God near Abraham. From time to time God appeared to Abraham as recorded in several places in Genesis. This does not mean that Abraham saw the full and complete glory of God, but it does mean that Abraham experienced God's close presence and an everlasting close friendship. In Genesis 18 the Son of God took a body which concealed enough of His glory that Abraham could survive in His presence and converse with Him. Such a friendship is infinitely more valuable to us and lasts longer than any relationship among imperfect human beings.

The friendship did not stop with the physical death of Abraham. If one reads again the encounter involving the rich man and Lazarus, Abraham appears. When the rich man asks for water to cool his burning tongue, Abraham tells him that it is impossible. When the rich man asks that someone be sent back to warn his 5 brothers not to come to the place where the rich man found himself, Abraham's answer was, *"They have Moses and the prophets. Let them hear them."* Luke 16:29. Consider this twice: how did Abraham know about Moses and the prophets? When Abraham walked the earth, Moses was more than 500 years in the future and the prophets were yet further in the future. It would be roughly 1000 years from Abraham to David, one of the earliest of the prophets. We can exclude any notion that Abraham had knowledge of Moses or the prophets from anything he learned while living on earth in a body of flesh and blood. Instead, Abraham continued to learn after his physical death as he remained in fellowship with his spiritual Father in heaven. From heaven Abraham observed and learned of Moses and of the prophets (see also Hebrews 12:1).

Abraham and Sarah had an exceptionally strong marriage which also is an example for every married Christian. To state the obvious, this marriage, like every marriage in the Bible, was between male and female. This was first established at Creation and confirmed by the Lord Jesus

(Matthew 19:4). We know from the Bible (Proverbs 21:9, 25:24, 27:15-16) that many marriages are dysfunctional, and experience certainly confirms this. But Abraham and Sarah functioned joyfully as a married couple. They had the joy of a son in their old age, when Abraham was 100 years old and Sarah 90. They lived together with barely a break (if any at all) from when they married in Ur of the Chaldees until Sarah died at age 127. We do not know the exact length of the marriage, but an estimate of 75 years is conservative. They lived through the loss of Abraham's father, the separation between Abraham and Lot, the trip to Egypt where Abraham told Sarah to conceal their marriage, the crisis over Ishmael whose roots lay in Sarah's poor advice to Abraham concerning Hagar, wanderings through the Promised Land, and countless minor problems such as finding enough grass and water for all the livestock. They lived in tents; their idea of a new house was a replacement tent as the old one wore out. For a new car they might have gotten a replacement riding animal. Yet we find that they had an enduring love for one another as we read though Genesis 12-22. We have already observed that Paul holds us Abraham as a model for Christian believers; Peter holds us Sarah as a model for Christian women in 1 Peter 3:4-7 and also instructs husbands:

> *But let [your beauty] be the hidden man of the heart, in that which is not corruptible, of a meek and quiet spirit, which is in the sight of God of great price. For after this manner in the old time the holy women also, who trusted in God, adorned themselves, being in subjection unto their own husbands: even as Sarah obeyed Abraham, calling him lord: whose daughters ye are, as long as ye do well, and are not afraid with any amazement.*

> *Likewise, ye husbands, dwell with them according to knowledge, giving honor unto the wife, as unto the weaker vessel, and as being heirs together of the grace of life; that your prayers be not hindered.*

It is important for a Christian wife to submit to her husband, but it is equally important for the husband to lead in the interests of the entire family and especially of his wife rather than in his own interest, subject to the paramount duty of obedience to God Himself. In Ephesians 5:24-25, we again find the twin commands to wives to submit to their husbands and to husbands to love their wives as Christ loved the church and gave Himself for it. Thus the command to a wife to submit is not an excuse for a dictatorial husband but rather lays the responsibility for wise and compassionate leadership on the husband, giving careful and prayerful consideration to the views of his wife. While within the Scriptures he has the power to overrule his wife's views, if the wife truly loves Christ he should exercise this authority only for substantial reasons. One would hope that such instances would be rare. In the modern age both responsibilities are scoffed at and disregarded. But they still are important ingredients for a joyful marriage, as they were for Abraham and Sarah. While they were not perfect, they were eminently successful. One counterpart marriage known in our age is the wonderful Christian marriage of Billy and Ruth Graham, contrasted to the destructive emotional turmoil and collapse of so many celebrity marriages such as that of Richard Burton and Elizabeth Taylor of the same era as the early years of the Graham marriage. I have seen marriages collapse because of failure to lead by the husband or refused submission by the wife. Sometimes parents of the groom or bride encourage the destructive patterns within the marriage. This type of slow-motion train wreck is gut-wrenching to watch—I know from personal and professional experience both from direct observation and from professional experience as an attorney who has handled many divorce cases. A husband leading his wife in love and purity in the manner that Jesus Christ leads His Church is a great start to a delightful and enduring marriage, especially if his wife responds with love and obedience from obedience and gratitude to God for saving her soul. But neither can expect the other to be perfect.

Theologians debate whether God as a holy God is bound by His own Law or whether He is free to set aside His law at his pleasure for His own good reasons. Some argue that God's holiness is a restriction on His sovereignty and reason that He Himself would never act contrary to His own laws. In response one would argue that God is totally sovereign first and foremost and that He has the right to do as He pleases. His holy character will direct His sovereignty but does not diminish that sovereignty. To resolve this, we must search the Scriptures.

In Isaiah 45:7 God said, *"I form the light and create darkness; I make peace and create evil. I the Lord do all these things."* Nebuchadnezzar, surely an expert on the human sovereignty of an absolute dictator in the first true great power in the Middle East, at the end of his life on earth said, *"I blessed the Most High and I praised and honored Him Who lives forever, Whose dominion is an everlasting dominion, and Whose kingdom is from generation to generation. And all the inhabitants of the earth are reputed as nothing, and He does according to His will in the army of heaven and the inhabitants of the earth, and none can stay His hand or say to him, "What are you doing? . . . Now I Nebuchadnezzar praise and extol and honor the King of Heaven, all Whose works are truth and His ways just, and all who walk in pride He is able to abase.* Daniel 4:34-5, 37. Then we read in Romans 9:15-18, *"For He says to Moses, 'I will have mercy on whom I will have mercy, and I will have compassion on whom I will have compassion.' So then it is not of him that wills, nor of him that runs, but of God Who shows mercy. For the Scripture says to Pharaoh, 'Even for this same purpose I have raised you up, that I might show My power in you, and that My name may be declared in all the earth.' Therefore He has mercy on whom He will, and whom He wills he hardens."* These are declarations of a God Who claims and exercises total sovereignty, including in the matter of the salvation or damnation of human beings. Thousands of years later, God is still exalted when considering the lives of Nebuchadnezzar and of Pharaoh, even though the outcome for Nebuchadnezzar was salvation and the outcome for Pharaoh was damnation. Both deserved damnation; Nebuchadnezzar received grace and mercy but Pharaoh did not. Isaiah himself expected to die when he saw heaven opened in Isaiah 6, but instead an angel spared him and purged him with a coal from the altar in heaven.

So far we have derived our expansive view of God's sovereignty from Scriptures that treat the issue in general terms. Can we confirm it with specific Biblical examples from Scripture? Deuteronomy 23:1-4 lists several classes of people excluded from the congregation of the Lord. Once the Temple had been constructed, they would have been excluded from Temple worship. One set of excluded men were those who had been castrated or were similarly emasculated. And yet in at least two instances God used such men. One saved Jeremiah from nearly certain death in the muddy bottom of a well. Jeremiah 38:1-13 gives the account. The other example is Daniel the prophet, who started his schooling as one of the eunuchs of Nebuchadnezzar (Daniel 1:3,7). This remarkable man was probably the greatest Secretary of the Treasury any government has ever had. More than that, he was one of the most faithful of the prophets of God, called "greatly beloved" in Daniel 10:11. Through faith Daniel remained at peace in the lions' den. Daniel was given more information about the political future of the world than any other prophet with the possible exception of the Apostle John and Revelation. Daniel's prayer life was one of unusual power. So God retained and used the power to set aside the Law excluding castrated men from worship in at least these two cases. The salvation of the Ethiopian eunuch in Acts 8:27-39 continues this pattern in the New Testament.

In Deuteronomy 23:2 people born out of wedlock and their descendants are excluded from the congregation of the Lord. Yet Jephthah (Judges 11) was used by God to set Israel free from attempted oppression by the children of Ammon, one of the peoples descended from Abraham's nephew Lot. He had been born out of wedlock and driven away from his family by the legitimate children. So Jephthah went to a lawless border area and led guerrilla raiders. These raiders were probably rejected men similar to Jephthah. Like David in later times when he fled from Saul, Jephthah got much of his military training as a guerrilla leader on the fringe of civilization. Today we have a similar situation in the northwest territories of Pakistan. When his brothers were helpless before the Ammonites, they wanted Jephthah back! Jephthah had true faith in God; God used Jephthah notwithstanding his tainted origins to set Israel free from oppression. Perhaps in using such a castoff God was sending a rebuke to Israel's designated leaders, who should have been leading in both worship and defense, that they had been doing a poor job or even had been unfaithful to God.

In Deuteronomy 23:3-6 we read that Moabites are among those excluded from the congregation of the Lord because they refused food and water to Israel on its way to the Promised Land. Did God ever set aside this prohibition? Yes, as the entire Book of Ruth shows. Ruth was a woman of Moab who had married an Israeli migrant to Moab. He had died. Ruth's sister was in a like situation. Naomi, Ruth's mother-in-law, urged Ruth to stay with her own people, but Ruth utterly refused. *"Where you go, I will go; where you lodge, I will lodge. Your people shall be my people, and your God my God. Where you die, I will die, and there shall I be buried."* Ruth

1:16-17. The children of Lot had become idolatrous by this time, but Ruth worshiped the God of Israel, not the god of the land of her birth.

Ruth's ancestry was from a forbidden nation according to Deuteronomy, but God received her anyhow. Ruth was given a wealthy husband of Israel in Bethlehem. Not only that, from Ruth and her husband Boaz came Obed, Jesse and one of the most important men for good in the history of the world, King David. Through King David Ruth became a human ancestress of incomparably the most important human being ever, the King of Kings Jesus the Messiah, the Son of God, Son of Man and Savior of the world.

Surely in Ruth's reception into the family of the Messiah we see the power and right of God to set aside His own law. We as human beings have no such authority on our own, but we must recognize His absolute authority to use whom He wills in the manner that He wills without ever being tainted with sin or impurity. As the Lord Jesus was able to disregard the Law and touch lepers to heal them and enter their dwellings without himself becoming unclean (Matthew 8:2-4; 26:6; Mark 1:40-42; 14:3), so His Father can metaphorically or literally touch the foulest life without Him partaking in that person's sins. Our God is not bound by rules, not even those which He has given us. If He were, we would all be doomed to damnation. As it is written, *"The soul that sins shall die."* Ezekiel 18:4. But our Lord Jesus was able to say truly to Martha, *"Whoever believes in Me shall never die. Do you believe this?"* John 11:26. Martha was expert in running a household rather than given to thought as was her sister Mary, but Martha gave the right answer, *"Yes, Lord. I believe that You are the Christ, the Son of God, Who is to come into the world."* John 11:27. Were our thoughts put through an autopsy in the manner of a body, we would merit not only death but damnation a million times over, but Martha's confession is the remedy for all that and more. *"The blood of Jesus Christ cleanses us from all sin."* 1 John 1:7.

We already have seen 3 examples where God overruled specific exclusions in Deuteronomy 23. One more example where God put aside guilt for both adultery and murder to use an adulterous couple should be sufficient to establish precedent from the Old Testament. Starting in 2 Samuel 11 we find the story of David and Bath-sheba. In 2 Samuel 7 God had promised David a son who would build a house (a temple) for God. Indeed the promise of a son went beyond the construction of what became known as Solomon's Temple. It also encompassed a Son Who would reign forever. When David received this promise, he had been married several times and had had male children. Speaking from a purely physical perspective, it was not necessary for David to marry again for God to fulfill His promise. But when we examine the Biblical record of 1 Chronicles 3 concerning the children of David, that record shows that none of the children that had been born to David up to that time was to be part of the succession. God used a relationship that could hardly have been started under worse circumstances as His chosen channel of *"the sure mercies of David."* (Isaiah 55:3, Acts 13:34)

For a full account of the facts, start reading in 2 Samuel 10. David was coming off high points in his life. He had succeeded in uniting the nation of Israel under his rule. The Ark of the Covenant had been successfully brought to Jerusalem amid great jubilation. God had made a covenant with David one night. Then David with great generosity had received his (now deceased) enemy Saul's grandson Mephibosheth into his court. Mephibosheth was not only a potential enemy because of his heredity, he also was handicapped to the extent that he could never serve as a soldier and probably could not even walk. David, like God, had shown mercy to the helpless.

The first detonation in the chain reaction of sin took place in Ammon, a territory bordering Israel on the east. The old king, who had had peaceful relations with David, had died. David had sent emissaries to the funeral and to the coronation of the new king. He provoked David by insulting the emissaries and by cutting half of their clothes and half of their beards. David responded to this mistreatment of his emissaries by declaring war and sending Joab, commander of the army, against the insolent new king. But David stayed behind and saw a woman named Bath-sheba while he was on his roof. She was already married to Uriah, one of David's top soldiers and leaders.

The sight of Bath-sheba so excited David that he summoned Bath-sheba to the palace for a tryst. She came without protest and then left. Matters might have rested there except that Bath-sheba became pregnant by David.

David's first idea was to have Uriah come home, expecting Uriah to enter his home and enjoy his wife while on leave. So he summoned Uriah home, but Uriah refused to enter his house and slept outside as his soldiers did at the front in Ammon. Since Uriah did not provide cover for David's adultery, David decided that Uriah had to die under circumstances that his death would appear to be a battle casualty. So David ordered Uriah to deliver a sealed order to Joab, ordering Joab to cause Uriah to die by leaving Uriah exposed during a tactical retreat. To a point, David's plan succeeded. Uriah did die in battle and Bath-sheba did come to David's palace as his new wife. David expected to get away with adultery and then murder, but God would have none of it. God exposed David's sin to Nathan the prophet, who then confronted David (2 Samuel 12).

One part of the sequel is the family conflict that David faced for the rest of his life on earth. David's first son by Bath-sheba died a week after birth. David's first-born son Amnon became inflamed over Tamar, his half-sister and full sister to Absalom, David's third son. Amnon made up a story about being sick, lured Tamar into his room, raped her and then ordered her out of his room like a piece of garbage. David failed to act, probably because he knew that his own sin was worse. Under the Law of Moses, Amnon deserved to die. When Absalom saw that his father did nothing, he took the law into his own hands. He invited Amnon to a party and had Amnon killed. Then Absalom fled the country for 3 years. Joab, the commander of David's army, then brokered an arrangement for Absalom's return with his father David's consent.

But Absalom was not content with returning to Israel as a prince. He wanted to overthrow his father and rule in his own right. So Absalom continued to harp on his father's lack of attention to justice (with probably a grain of truth) with the purpose of stoking a revolution, which indeed he tried. For about 3 months he appeared to succeed, but then was killed in the decisive battle when his own long hair got caught in a tree. Joab personally finished him off.

In the last year of David's life Adonijah tried to take the throne, but David, Bath-sheba and Nathan the prophet together crushed this putsch and secured Solomon's succession. Adonijah was eventually executed by Solomon shortly after David's death. So in total four sons of David died unnatural deaths: the baby, Bath-sheba's first-born son by David; Amnon; Absalom; and Adonijah. Tamar's life was probably wrecked; we hear nothing more about her after the rape. In this branch of the history David reaped what he sowed in his family. As Nathan the prophet told David, *"Now therefore the sword shall never turn aside from your house, because you have despised Me and taken the wife of Uriah the Hittite to be a wife for yourself."* 2 Samuel 12:10 (based on the literal translation).

But this is not the whole story. Along with these judgments, there were also the mercies of God coming through David's marriage to Bath-sheba. David already had several wives and children, but none of those already born were to be the children through whom God's covenant promises to David were to be fulfilled. From reading 1 Chronicles 3, it seems also that David went from woman to woman without being satisfied with any of them as a mate. Each wife then with David had one male child and no more. When we come to Bath-sheba (Bath-shua) in 1 Chronicles 3:5, we see no less than 4 male children. That indicates a long-term marital relationship between the two and also may be God's full replacement for the children that He took away to discipline David because of his sin. At the end of David's life, it was Bath-sheba who was still there with Nathan the Prophet (not to be confused with Nathan, one of the children of David and Bath-sheba listed in 1 Chronicles 3:5 who is part of the lineage of the Lord Jesus in Luke 3:31) to support David in securing Solomon's succession to the throne. It is remarkable that Bath-sheba maintained close relations with the very prophet who had denounced David's sin with her. She was not only forgiven but became a woman of exceptional spiritual quality.

In the immediate context, God used Bath-sheba to bear and train Solomon, the wisest man ever to live short of Jesus Christ. From Solomon come major portions of the Old Testament. By Solomon's testimony, that started with David and Bath-sheba: *"My son, listen to the instruction of your father and do not forsake the law of your mother."* Proverbs 1:8.

Later in history, God chose to bring both branches of the ancestry of Jesus Christ through David and Bath-sheba. There was no physiological necessity for this. God had other choices and could have created more choices, but He chose deliberately David and Bath-sheba jointly for this notwithstanding the awful sin in which their relationship started. I do not know all of God's purposes for this, but I can see that God is showing His forgiveness and blessing in the same lives as His severe corrective discipline as a model for every Christian to study. We see both the discipline and the forgiveness of God to the believer. Even those of us who have not sinned in the same way that David and Bath-sheba did still need both the discipline and the forgiveness of God continually as He knows how to express both in each redeemed life. *"Where sin did abound, grace did much more abound."* Romans 5:20.

So we can see in the lives of David and Bath-sheba the sovereign choice of God to make them jointly a channel for the blessing of every nation and tribe under heaven through Jesus Christ, the Son of David. If God had applied His Law without clemency, both would have been executed. But through the mercy of God they lived to be a supreme blessing first to Israel and then to the whole human race. Since there was forgiveness for them, there can be forgiveness to any who will pray honestly like the tax collector: *"God, be merciful to me a sinner."* Luke 18:13.

As one meditates on David and Bath-sheba, it is natural to wrestle with the question of when to forgive and when to refuse. If every sin of every person were forgiven without condition, holiness would have no meaning and unholiness would never have any consequences. When dealing with fellow human beings, there is the natural fear that forgiveness may simply make the offender feel as if he or she has gotten away with sin. We have already seen that God forgave Nebuchadnezzar but condemned Pharaoh. If we were to move forward to Romans 9, we would see that God forgave Jacob but damned Esau and that these decisions were predestined before the twins were born (Romans 9:11). Neither deserved forgiveness. One could make similar comparisons elsewhere in Scripture. Among evil kings, Ahab of the Northern Kingdom died under the judgment of God while Manasseh of Judah received forgiveness late in life when his reign had probably been even worse than that of Ahab. So if God forgives some and rebuffs others, how do we know whether to forgive or rebuff when we are wronged ourselves or see others wronged?

Our dealings with others will never be perfect. However, we can observe with James that *"God resists the proud but gives grace to the humble."*

James 4:6. So in imitation of God we should be more inclined to forgive the humble and penitent one. *"If he repents, forgive him."* Luke 17:3. In Matthew 18:15-22, we are instructed to forgive repeatedly within the Church. The Apostle Paul went so far as to instruct that it is better to be defrauded by a church brother than to sue a brother in secular courts. 1 Corinthians 6:1-8. Paul's other preferred method to settle disputes was by mediation or arbitration by someone wise within the Body of Christ. Clearly, it is easier to pass over a transgression and absorb the wrong if we ourselves are the only injured party than if others will be hurt as well.

Another principle of guidance, taken from the Old Testament, is whether forgiveness will establish a precedent which will encourage others to sin in the future. One sees a principle of public rebuke when an elder sins in 1 Timothy 5:20 and also a principle under the Old Covenant that the Law must be enforced lest others be encouraged to offend because someone "got away with it." Deuteronomy 13:11, 21:21. We should also remember that when God forgives that He also corrects and chastens (for example, Hebrews 12). He does not ignore the sin; rather He chooses to correct it instead of imposing the full penalty of eternal death.

Even if we believe that in good conscience that we cannot pass over a transgression, we must forgive the offender in our hearts and pray for his or her restoration or transformation. Vengeance is God's prerogative, not ours. Both the Lord Jesus and Stephen had the same essential prayer for their executioners: *"Father, forgive them, for they do not know what they do."* Luke 23:34 *"Lay not this sin to their charge."* Acts 7:60. Just after the Lord's Prayer, the Lord Jesus warned that we refuse to forgive that our Father will refuse to forgive us.

(In time of war, different principles apply when dealing with enemies who are still fighting. At least toward active combatants, the issues are so bitter that outward expression of forgiveness must await surrender. As a practical matter, a decisive victory early will spare many more lives later that would be lost in a long war. A full discussion of the theology of war is beyond our scope here, but the Bible as a whole discourages war especially for minor causes without forbidding it entirely.)

Moving forward to Jesus Christ, one could analyze His humane interpretation of the Fourth Commandment concerning the sabbath and contrast it to the legalistic interpretation of the Pharisees, but there is a more radical example of His willingness to set aside the Law, even though the Law was good and holy (Romans 7:12), for mercy's sake. This is the case of the woman with a perpetual flow of blood for 12 years, which made her perpetually unclean. (For the legal reference, review Leviticus 15, especially 15:25. For the complete Gospel accounts, see Matthew 9:20-22; Mark 5:25-34; and Luke 8:43-48.) As an unclean woman she was required to maintain continuous separation from other people, like a leper. She sought in vain for a medical cure and exhausted her money in the process. There seemed to be nothing left to her but to wait for death, like a modern cancer patient for whom nothing more can be done. In leaving her place of isolation this woman was violating every specific Old Testament law covering her condition in a desperate attempt to see the Lord Jesus and to touch the tassels of His rabbinical robe. She correctly perceived in Him the power to heal and so she went for broke in faith, violating the Law of Leviticus 15. She left behind any respectability she had left for this one attempt in faith to get the attention of the Great Physician. She even plunged into a crowd, brushing countless people, while under a legal injunction to touch no one, all to get to the Lord Jesus. Finally she pushed her way through and was able to reach His tassels and was instantly healed. Her violations of the Law were not even mentioned. A further point is that in her case, as in the cases where the Lord Jesus touched and healed lepers, the Law was actually reversed. By Law, the Lord Jesus Himself should have become unclean by touching or being touched by an unclean person. Instead, the unclean person became clean and the Lord Jesus remained clean as He always was. This is a tiny illustration of how sin is not just transferred to the sacrificial animal as under the Old Covenant but is extinguished completely, as will be the case in the resurrection (or rapture) and the Last Judgment.

So as Christians we have to walk a narrow way between wicked lawlessness (. . . *sin is the transgression of the Law.* I John 3:4) and a rigid legalism that never admit to exceptions to the Law. Jesus Christ was *"made of a woman, made under the Law."* Galatians 4:4. Yet He from time to time set the Law aside and certainly did not conform to the prevailing interpretation of the Law. Also, we cannot exclude forgiveness in our own lives (see Matthew 18:21-35) and certainly we cannot oppose God when He forgives, as Jonah tried to do when he tried to run away from God's commission to Nineveh. We can neither obey the Law perfectly nor always know when to set the strictures of the Law aside. We do not have God's authority to change the Law. Nevertheless, we can improve as we become better acquainted with the Bible and more attuned to the Holy Spirit. Prayer helps greatly too. We can gradually become better reflections of our Lord and Master, Jesus Christ.

CHAPTER 2

Holiness, Vigilance & Prayer

The concept of "watch" is scattered through the Holy Scriptures. Ezekiel wrote of the duties of a watchman in both Ezekiel 3 and in Ezekiel 33. In the military, a sentry must stay awake and remain alert to the stealthy approach of an enemy. Top naval submarine commanders spared no effort in improving their crew's night vision so that vigilance would have its maximum impact. As Christians, the analogy is obvious. We must remain awake and sober spiritually. We must also read and digest the Scriptures and to pray as the submariners used to eat oatmeal and carrots and also wear red goggles below-decks to sharpen their physical sight at night. As to the command of the Lord Jesus to watch, look at Matthew 24:42-4 and 25:13 and then the inability of the disciples to obey recorded in Matthew 26:38-41.

In this Internet age, some people hire technological experts to help them keep watch over their financial accounts to prevent identity theft. Others check their financial accounts frequently if they have the time and skill to do so. Either way, this vigilance in earthly matters is a counterpart of the vigilance (or watchfulness) that we need to live out in spiritual matters also. Yes, we do need physical sleep in peace because God is always watching over us (Psalm 121:4), but in spiritual matters we must remain awake and watchful (1 Peter 4:7).

For what are we to watch? The Lord Jesus gives us an answer in Matthew 16:2-3: *"When it is evening, you say, 'Fair weather,' for the sky is red. And in the morning, 'Foul weather today,' for the sky is red and glowering. O hypocrites, you can discern the face of the sky, but can you not [discern] the signs of the times?"* So we are to be reading the signs of the times in societies around us. And what do we see? In France, there is a President who has had four children with a woman whom he never married and is now living with another woman without benefit of marriage. In the United States, there are strong movements to make polygamy and same-sex marriages legal throughout the United States. Abortions occur around the world for many reasons, including sex selection to avoid the future expense of providing a dowry for a girl or for personal convenience. Some governments have used abortions for population control. Mind-bending drugs have multiplied. Cocaine, justly feared for its addictive powers, seems almost passé in this era of *krokodil* (with intense cravings and effects something like fleshing-eating staph infections that can be fatal, with its worst effects so far in Russia), of bath salts and of crystal methamphetamine. There is now a growing movement to make marijuana legal for general use. Ponzi schemes have proliferated since the original in the 1920s. Stealing, especially by Internet and by paper, has become endemic. If you look at Revelation 9:21, you can see that we have touched upon the four major sins which humanity as a whole refuses to surrender no matter how much pressure God applies. Reading the spiritual "weather," the sky is red and glowering, portending a storm. Will this storm be confined to particular places or will it extend to the entire world and indeed into the whole universe? God has carefully concealed the time that the Lord Jesus will return for judgment, but the spiritual signs are so ominous that they look more like a figurative tornado line than a simple thunderstorm. As the disciples should have done in the Garden, we must *"Watch and pray, that we do not enter into temptation."* Matthew 26:41.

Prayer is part of the duty of every Christian capable of it. Very few are exempt: those who are unconscious or too weak in mind or body to pray may be excused from this duty. Some pray more readily than others, but this is one duty shared by virtually all Christians. The Lord Jesus gave us the Lord's Prayer within the Sermon on the Mount as one model for prayer. While repeating this prayer and actually paying attention to its petitions is not wrong, our Lord gave it to us as one example of prayer and not as a mantra for mindless or hypnotic repetition. In John 17 we find the prayer of the Lord Jesus for the future Church about to be born through His death and resurrection. The Apostle Paul incorporated several prayers into his letters; some can be found in Ephesians 3:14-21, 2 Corinthians 13:7, Philippians 1:9-11, Colossians 1:9-15 (just where the prayer stops and where the teaching resumes is not totally clear to me); and 1 Thessalonians 5:23. Paul also prayed for the forgiveness of those who did not stand in his defense (2 Timothy 4:16) in a way that echoes Stephen's prayer for his executioners (Acts 7:60) and the prayer of the Lord Jesus for his executioners (Luke 23:34). Very few of us if any can pray with this degree of intensity, but that does not excuse failure to pray at all or even failure to make prayer a recurring theme in our lives. We should pray for our own needs, but one will see that the Lord Jesus and Paul both concentrated on the needs of others. Paul directed that prayer be made for all kinds of people, even including bad politicians. 1 Timothy 2:1-4. I am not excusing the failures of modern rulers, but Nero—one of the worst ever—was probably the Emperor when 1 Timothy was written. If not, then it was Claudius, who was also twisted to a lesser degree than the infamous Nero. If God commanded prayer for them, He equally commands prayer for current rulers notwithstanding their sins. The Holy Spirit knew that we would need encouragement to pray, and so He says, *"For we do not have a High Priest [Jesus Christ] Who cannot be touched with our weaknesses, but Who was in all points tempted as we are, yet without sin. Therefore let us come boldly to the throne of grace, that we may obtain mercy and obtain grace to help in time of need."* Hebrews 4:15-16.

In addition to watching our world around us, we need to examine our own souls for sinful attitudes as a nation at war would be vigilant against enemy spies and traitors among its own citizens. Indeed the enemy of our souls seeks to do as much damage as he can, using our own internal sin as his weapon. Sin will even use a valid commandment of God to try to bludgeon us to death (Romans 7:11). Faith in the sacrifice and forgiveness of Jesus Christ is our shield against this form of attack.

In connection with the Lord's Supper, Paul instructs us through the Holy Spirit, *"Let a person examine himself [or herself] and so eat of that bread and drink of that cup."* 1 Corinthians 11:28. Paul again zeroes in on our thoughts in Romans 6:11, *"Account yourself to be dead indeed to sin but alive to God through Jesus Christ our Lord."* As one watches in prayer, one can remember the prayer of David, *"Search me, O God, and know my heart; try me and know my thoughts; and see if [there is] any wicked way within me, and lead me in the way everlasting."* Psalm 139:23-24.

The end of this 2-front war will come, but not while we remain in this body. In the meantime, holiness requires that we stand watch concerning our society, our family as did Job, our friends (once again, Job did this as he was restored) and our own soul. May God give us strength and endurance.

CHAPTER 3

⸺◦⸺

Holy and Polluted Love

English has one word for love. The Beatles in English could sing "All you need is love" without being specific as to what kind or quality of love was meant. If the word "love" is used indiscriminately, the Beatles' song becomes a monstrous lie, meaning that any sort of love will be sufficient for a good life. Greek, the language of the New Testament, has three different words covering portions of our single English word. *Eros* covers sexual love. *Phileo* covers fellowship, such as family fellowship or fellowship within a healthy military unit. *Agape* deals with self-sacrificial love, with its highest example being the voluntary death of the Lord Jesus Christ on behalf of His people to become the ransom for their sins. C.S. Lewis portrayed this in his book *Chronicles of Narnia* through the death of the lion; this was made into a modern movie. Each of these forms of love, absent disability, should be present in a healthy marriage. Each of these forms of love can be and too often are polluted and turned to poison. Hence a part of the title of this chapter: *Polluted Love.*

When we speak of the quality or purity of love, an analogy to drinking water will be helpful. Very few of us drink absolutely pure water with all other substances absent. Water on earth must be specially distilled to reach this state of 100% purity. Similarly, except with Jesus Christ there is no human love of any kind that is absolutely pure and free from sin. So for the present time when we speak of love on earth, as with drinking water we mean love (or water) of sufficient purity so as to be healthy without implying absolute purity. With drinking water, we have limits for certain substances that are known to be unhealthy in significant quantity, such as arsenic and many other substances and also potentially dangerous organisms such as *e coli*. Almost all of us drink water which has some level of contaminants, but not sufficient to cause substantial health hazards. Love at its best on the present earth is like healthy but not absolutely pure drinking water. On the other hand, when we speak of love in heaven, love before the fall into sin of Satan and then of Adam and Eve; or love from God the Father, from Jesus Christ the Son of God or from the Holy Spirit, we are then speaking of absolutely pure love. This should be understood throughout this book even though we do not have a separate word to designate absolutely pure divine love.

One can also infer this from the fact that after the original sin of Adam and Eve there has been no sinless person on the earth apart from Jesus Christ. The presence of sin makes all forms of even healthy love impure and imperfect. Apart from Jesus Christ, is there anyone who has complied with the distilled form of the law found in Mark 12:30 and in Luke 10:27? The French have a good answer to this: <<*Mille fois non!*>>—a thousand times no! There is not one person—emphatically including this author—who loves the Lord his God will all of his heart, with all of his soul, with all of his mind and with all of his strength. Romans 3:10-18 begins its climax of the indictment of the human race with this gloomy but realistic observation: *"There is none righteous—no, not one."* Romans 3:10, referring to Psalm 14:1-3 and Psalm 53:1-3. Even believers made alive by the Spirit of God, including the Apostle John himself, must confess: *"If we say we have no sin, we deceive ourselves and the truth is not in us."* 1 John 1:8. This means that we are incapable of sinless love, although the human race is capable of enough love to maintain civilization as opposed to chaos even in the state of spiritual death. However, we all as originally conceived and born are incapable of spiritual righteousness and must be delivered by God from our sin. Ephesians 2:1-10 is probably the strongest passage on this subject. John 3 also makes this clear. Until we are completely free from sin after our resurrection, our love will never be completely pure even though it may bear the character of one or more of the three kinds of Biblical love.

Dealing with erotic love, God through His Word is explicit that this love can only be expressed rightly in a marriage between one man and one woman. When this principle is honored, erotic love acts as a great binding force helping to hold a marriage together. While there has been a recurring theme in religious and other literature that erotic love is somehow spiritually suspect, erotic love within a marriage is a great good for the marriage regardless of the age of the couple and in fact necessary for the conception and birth of children, which is one purpose of most marriages of younger couples. Without erotic love, the human race would become extinct.

Any experienced homicide detective can give numerous examples of the explosive force of erotic love gone bad. Some television networks make a living at portraying such cases. As I first composed this in May 2013, the Jodi Arias case was drawing a multitude of viewers not normally watching legal channels. The Linda Broderick case is still famous in Southern California. After she was divorced, she shot in bed her ex-husband and his lover who had become his second wife. The O.J. Simpson case is still another infamous example. God had every reason to command against adultery in the Seventh Commandment.

The love of fellowship can also be corrupted. Consider the example of the Hitler Youth that fought ferociously in Normandy. Reading the historical accounts from the Allied side, there can be no doubt about their zeal and their skill. Their military cohesion was extremely high. So in a limited sense there can be no doubt that the Hitler Youth troops in Normandy showed *phileo*. But this *phileo* became perverse because the fellowship was corrupted by the dreadful regime that the young men served. What might have been admirable in service of a better cause became execrable because the young men were fighting for a murderous regime. This military fellowship had to be broken for the sake of the entire human race no matter what potentially admirable qualities might have been present in the individual soldiers.

One cannot separate fully an emotion from its object or from the cause which the emotion serves. Consider the undoubted intelligence and courage of Admiral Yamamoto of Japan during World War 2. His very qualities that made him a skilled warrior also made him a special target of the United States Navy. On a far greater scale, the coming Anti-Christ will be a skilled leader and diplomat and will have a higher intelligence than even Daniel the prophet (Ezekiel 28:3 referring to Satan directly but probably also to the Anti-Christ who will be filled with Satan and act as Satan on earth). This will make the Anti-Christ a special target of the returning Jesus Christ, acting with all the power and authority of God Almighty.

For present purposes, the implication is that love must be assessed not only for its intrinsic quality but also by the object of that love. Love serves something or someone. The Lord Jesus said, *"Whosoever would be chief among you, let him be your servant."* Matthew 20:27; see also Matthew 23:11. Yamamoto was serving an ideology that made a false god of the Emperor of Japan. Consider also the recent case of the Austrian father who committed repeated incest with his daughter. No matter the quality or strength of the erotic feelings of this father toward his daughter, they are utterly corrupt because the erotic feelings are directed at a forbidden object. One could and should make the same observation of homoerotic feelings or erotic feelings directed toward a person of the opposite sex who is already married to someone else. And any married person is similarly forbidden to entertain erotic feeling toward anyone not his wife. To be healthy, any form of love must be aimed in a direction permitted by God.

Even *agape* love can be corrupted. According to Ephesians 5:22-33, the closest example of the love of Christ for His Bride is the love of a husband for his wife. If necessary, the man is willing to give himself for his wife. Some of the male passengers on the <u>Titanic</u> actually did this, seeing that their wives escaped even though it meant that they would go down with the ship. Bonnie and Clyde together form an illustration of a corrupt form of this type of love, as they joined together to commit robbery and sometimes murder in the process. In medieval history, Henry Plantagenet of England and Eleanor of Aquitaine were a somewhat similar pair seeking power by joining their domains through marriage, without discounting that they probably did care for one another at the start of their relationship. As with *phileo*, it is possible to have *agape* love between a man and a woman in order to take from others rather than to give glory to God. If there is *agape* love between Satan and the Anti-Christ, such love would be absolutely corrupt because of the vile object and objective of that relationship. This would be polluted love.

For holy love to exist, the object and purpose of the love must be holy and the method of expression must also be holy. This is possible between Christ and the believer, among believers and between husband and wife. I can also imagine *phileo* love that at least has positive aspects outside the church. Family love is a prominent example. Fellowship in a workplace, in a military or police force, in a team or in a student body would be another set of examples. Sexual love within monogamous heterosexual marriages even outside the church is healthy. But today's world insists on flaunting polluted love in both sexual and non-sexual terms. One example of non-sexual polluted love is that among conspirators to steal money by financial lies (although one recent example had a sexual component combined with misuse of insider information). Another is among conspirators to earn money distributing mind-altering drugs.

Corrupt love in all of its forms triggers the wrath of God. Romans 1:17-18 twice contained in English the word "revealed", once applying to the righteousness of God to save the faithful and once applying to the wrath of God against all unrighteous behavior. Prominent in the following specific description of unrighteous behavior are several sexual sins. Both same-sex and opposite-sex sins outside of Biblical marriage between one man and one woman are denounced severely along with other non-sexual sins that also make God angry.

The word "revealed" is the same Greek word from which we get the Apocalypse, which is an alternate title for the book of Revelation written by the Apostle John. In overview, Paul reveals in detail both the righteousness of God in ransoming His people and the righteousness of God in judging and destroying the remainder of the human race. Paul's presentation speaks especially to people who reach truth through logic and reasoning and draws extensively on the Old Testament. Like Isaiah, Paul will reason with his readers. John's Book of Revelation deals extensively with the redemption of God's people and the wrath of God against unbelievers. It also draws extensively on the Old Testament. But John's presentation is predominantly visual. The original form in which John received this truth was a movie. With the full inspiration of the Holy Spirit, John wrote it for preservation through centuries which lacked technological means to preserve and transmit visual material in visual form. But John's presentation, like Ezekiel's and Daniel's prophecies before, appeals especially to visually oriented people. Despite the different methods of presentations, the essential messages are the same. Polluted love frequently provokes the wrath of God, whether in the lives of individuals, nations or even the entire human race. It will ultimately provoke the destruction of our current civilization and the everlasting destruction of billions from the presence of the Lord. 2 Thessalonians 1:8-9.

Let's go back in time to see some of the effect of sin on once pure love in the case of Adam and Eve. When they were first created, they loved each other in absolute purity and in perfect harmony with God. Adam and Eve had had direct fellowship with God when He walked in the Garden of Eden (Genesis 3:8). They had erotic love for each other with no self-consciousness (Genesis 2:25). At this early stage before sin, there was no need of sacrificial *agape* love because there was as yet no sin, aging, scarcity or death. All of those came later in Genesis 3 as part of the Fall.

Next we should consider the impact of the Fall on the relationship between Adam and Eve. They would have delighted one another to a degree that we cannot fully imagine today when we must combat both internal and external sin. Both Adam and Eve were able to speak directly to God and to receive communication directly from God as human beings converse with one another today. At this stage there was but one human language, which continued until the Tower of Babel in Genesis 11. Adam and Eve could eat well simply by taking fruit from the fruit trees in the Garden of Eden, with the exception of one forbidden tree. If there were any direct contact between Satan and either Adam or Eve, it would have been in perfect harmony with the purpose of God as part of Satan's (probably then known as Lucifer) light-bearing responsibilities in connection with the worship of God by all Creation. I think it more likely that Lucifer would have functioned in the background so far as Adam and Eve were concerned. (Read Isaiah 14 and Ezekiel 28 for as much information as we have about Lucifer before the Fall.) Among God, Adam and Eve there was then perfect harmony and no blemish of any kind. We cannot fully imagine the intellectual and emotional intimacy of this holy love triangle, nor the physical intimacy between Adam and Eve as husband and wife.

With the Fall, fatigue, aging and ultimately death enter all of creation, including marriage. There is now the need for clothing. God did provide the original skins for Adam and Eve to wear (Genesis 3:21) but thereafter clothing would have to be replenished. Since Adam was now required to raise crops (Genesis 3:17-19), he and his descendants would now need a variety of implements such as scythes and plows and eventually leather for use in hitching animals and perhaps for clothing. And so we read in Genesis 4 the rise of specialized occupations along with the progeny of Adam and Eve.

More than this, sin took an immediate deadly turn within the immediate family of Adam and Eve. Cain became jealous of God's acceptance of Abel's offering and expressed that jealousy by murdering Abel. (As a social aside, one should note that murder precedes the existence of any specialized instruments of death, whether swords, guns or other weapons. Control of weapons will not eradicate murder and may well be a springboard to monopolize and concentrate murder instead of to prevent it. Consider Hitler's Germany or Stalin's Russia as historical examples.) So we have a very early example of love between brothers (*phileo*) polluted to the point of being fatally toxic. Never again could the children of Adam relate to one another without a certain degree of wariness.

Adam and Eve now had to relate to uncounted children and their descendants with their specialized occupations, now necessary for the survival and spread of the human race. The possibilities for conflict grew exponentially. Prices were now necessary to permit exchange of labor and goods. It became possible for two men to want to marry the same woman or for two women to compete to marry the same man. A particular man or women might be deemed undesirable. Boundary conflicts within agriculture became possible. Even music could become a source of dispute. Adam and Eve must have been shocked by the collateral consequences of their first sin in terms of human relations as well as in their own bodies.

Marriage also deteriorated in the pre-Flood world of sin. We cannot be sure what exactly was meant when Genesis 6:2 informs us that the "sons of God" married the "daughters of men." It is clear enough that something awful happened to marriage. One possibility is that fallen angels were somehow able to marry human women and were able to sire giants. This would fit Old Testament usage but would at least be in tension with the teaching of our Lord Jesus recorded at Matthew 22:23-32, Mark 12:18-27 and Luke 20:26-38. As the Lord Jesus pointed out, angels as a rule do not marry, although His reference was specifically to the angels in heaven. Could there have been an exception allowed by God in Genesis 6 for fallen angels, as distinct from the holy angels in heaven (explicitly so in Matthew 22:39 and Mark 12:25 and reasonably so understood in Luke 20:36) of whom our Lord Jesus spoke? I cannot exclude this possibility even though it is foreign to our own experience. If this happened before the Flood, I am not aware of any evidence of repetition afterward even though we do encounter races of giants who were enemies of Israel as late as the time of Goliath's sons during David's reign. Perhaps it is the fallen angels who had mingled with human women who are chained in darkness as stated in Jude 6 (possibly with other fallen angels also). An argument can be made for this from the closeness to Jude 7, referring to the pervasive sexual sins of Sodom and Gomorrah. I am inclined to believe that fallen angels did impregnate human women in Genesis 6; the offspring would have died in the Flood. Since the Bible leaves some mystery here, we cannot be certain.

But it is obvious from Genesis 6:1-6 that some form of tampering with marriage angered God to the point where He was prepared to exterminate His own created human race. We have an obvious example of fatally toxic, polluted love. At least Enoch, already translated to heaven without death, would have been salvaged and others as well who had *"call[ed] on the name of the Lord."* Genesis 4:26. But instead of total extermination there was to be one family spared—that of Noah who had *"found grace in the eyes of the Lord."* Genesis 6:8.

We can consider briefly the Tower of Babel as another expression of polluted love. Nothing here is said about marriage or about erotic love. But the cooperation necessary for the construction of that tower speaks of highly developed *phileo* love and cooperation at the worksite. The trouble was that the purpose of the Tower was wicked as a human attempt to reach heaven. I infer that the ultimate and perhaps unspoken purpose of reaching heaven was to overthrow God with alliance with Satan, formerly Lucifer. But even if that inference is going too far, the Tower of Babel is an emblem of human efforts to reach heaven by human abilities as opposed to human acceptance of God's prescribed method of reaching heaven through God's grace and faith. This is humanity defying God instead of seeking reconciliation with a superior God against Whom we have sinned. The cooperation among people might have been admirable for other purposes but it became poisonous when harnessed to this purpose. So God introduced various languages to prevent such sinful cooperation again and He also divided the continents (Genesis 10:25) to make such a united project physically impossible.

To once again make the point that the ultimate objective is important in assessing whether a particular expression of love is good or not, contrast the Tower of Babel with the construction of Solomon's Temple described in 1 Kings 6. There was a high degree of organization and teamwork. For example, the stones were shaped at the quarry so that no tool would be used at the construction site out of reverence for God. Instead of the clattering of jackhammers and other power tools at a modern urban building site, there was virtual silence at the Temple sustained by a dedicated team of supervisors, foremen and workers committing to the worship of God even in the manner of the Temple's construction. This instance of workplace *phileo* was pleasing to the Lord, in contrast to the Tower of Babel, because the purpose was the worship of God instead of rebellion against Him in trying to build a tower to heaven.

If I had to pick but one Biblical example of poisonous erotic love, I would choose Samson. He should be a warning to every servant of God of the reality of sexual temptation and that even the strongest can be corrupted through illicit sex. In the late 20th century both Jim Bakker and Jimmy Swaggart were trapped in this way. This theme with variations has wound in and out of both human and Biblical history. An instance of this was the immediate cause of the beheading of John the Baptist, as recorded in Matthew 14:1-12 and in Mark 6:17-28. *"Lust, when it has conceived, brings forth sin. Sin, when it is finished, brings forth death."* James 1:15.

At this point we should focus on Samson as a vivid example of sexual temptation. He was attracted to Philistine women instead of to any woman of Israel. Judges 14:3-4. His parents were right to question this (Exodus 34:15-16 and Deuteronomy 7:3-4), not knowing that God was going to use Samson's sinful desires for His own purposes. After the failure of his marriage, Samson was left with a major hole in his life which he tried to fill with a prostitute (Judges 16:1-3) and finally with Delilah (starting with Judges 16:4). But these longings in the end led Samson to violate his covenant with God as expressed in his hair, which in turn led to Samson's being captured, blinded, enslaved and hitched like a beast of burden at a mill. But it did not stop even there. Eventually Samson died in the rubble of the Philistine structure which he pulled down.

Many of the Philistines who used Delilah to capture Samson likewise ended up dead in the same disaster. Their meddling with perverted love left them as dead as Samson and probably worse off. Samson with all of his flaws died a hero of faith (Hebrews 11:32). The Philistine nobles who used Delilah as their sexual bait to catch Samson probably ended up dead and facing the wrath of God forever. The false worship in Judges 16:23 is a clear indication of the Philistines' disbelief in the true God. We do not know whether Delilah herself died at the same party or whether she heard of the disaster and had an opportunity to reflect on the results of her own conduct (assuming that she was not already dead). But we do know that this is a cardinal example of the Scripture that the Holy Spirit gave to James, the half-brother of our Lord Jesus: *"Lust, when it is conceived, brings forth sin. Sin, when it is finished, brings forth death."* James 1:15. In this case, the dead mounted up into the thousands, all stemming from the polluted love between Samson and Delilah.

As a contrast to Samson and Delilah, consider the marriage of Joseph and Mary, the biological mother and adoptive father of Jesus of Nazareth, the Son of God. Joseph was gravely concerned about Mary's pregnancy despite the fact that before and during their engagement they had not had sexual relations with each other. In fact both were virgins, but Joseph needed a dream from God to understand that. So their marriage started the right way. They stayed together through the flight to Egypt ahead of Herod's murderous soldiers, their exile in Egypt and their return to Galilee. When God sent dreams to this Joseph (like his Old Testament namesake), Joseph obeyed God and Mary followed Joseph. When the Lord Jesus went to the Temple at about age 12, both Joseph and Mary went with Him. Here the records stops as to Joseph, although we learn in Mark 6:3 that the Lord Jesus had 4 half-brothers and at least 2 half-sisters. This indicates that after the Lord Jesus was born (see Matthew 1:24-25) Joseph and Mary enjoyed their relationship as husband and wife in both *eros* and *phileo* as well as in *agape*. This marriage, like that of Abraham and Sarah, is worthy of imitation as an example of holy though imperfect love.

CHAPTER 4

─◦◦◦─

Holiness at Home as a Foundation of Ministry

I remember at least two vivid instances illustrating how important 1 Timothy 3 and Titus 1 are in stressing the training that most pastors and deacons should experience as they lead their homes. One of them occurred over 30 years ago. An experienced police detective had retired and become a pastor of a church in a community new to him. When he and his wife came, he had as a church secretary a younger married woman of long standing in the community. I do not know what was happening between the new pastor and his wife, but it became common knowledge that the pastor and his secretary were having an affair. When it was exposed, the pastor committed suicide by shooting himself. I attended the wake and was amazed at the grace of the pastor's wife as she talked freely with his paramour. From anything I could see, she had forgiven the adulteress, following in the footsteps of the Lord Jesus who forgave the woman caught in adultery in John 8. But we should not overlook the obvious lesson that the pastor's adultery had destroyed his ministry even before he took his own life. And the tragedy in all likelihood did substantial harm to the church and to the witness of Jesus Christ in that community, although I was not inside the church to see the specifics.

The second instance is more recent and less drastic. I remember attending a newly formed church with two teaching pastors. The younger pastor was especially gifted in expounding and explaining the stories of the Old Testament. His wife seemed strongly moved by the worship and music of the service, to the point that it seemed that something was unusual. There were no children. About a year later, the pastor and his wife split apart and both left the church. So far as I know, the pastor moved to another state and then remarried, but his ministry where I had known him was destroyed. I do not know how either are faring now, but from the wording of 1 Timothy 3 and Titus 1 the young preacher can no longer serve as a pastor or deacon regardless of why his first marriage broke apart. This was a real loss to the church; I can only hope that the former pastor finds a way to serve the Lord Jesus suitable to his gifts from God.

I have dealt with Christian principles of marriage in more detail in several of my previous books, especially *Assault on Marriage: A Christian Response,* Trafford Press, 2012 and in Part IV of *Fighting the Good Fight,* Trafford Press, 2011. Therefore I will attempt only a bare summary of Christian teaching on marriage here. There is no obligation to marry, but only a select few have the ability to live as a single adult before old age. Marriage is to be monogamous between one man and one woman. Sexual relations are exclusively within the marriage relationship and should be only after the wedding. There is no such thing as an appropriate sexual relationship outside of an existing heterosexual, monogamous marriage. In principle, only physical death should sever a marriage, although the Bible does allow divorce in the cases of adultery (Matthew 19:1-12 is the leading passage) and of desertion (1 Corinthians 7 is the main passage.) Widows are permitted to remarry. Under Old Testament civil law, divorced people were permitted to remarry (Deuteronomy 24:1-4, but within the Church consideration must also be given to Matthew 5:31-32; I will by-pass any attempt to expound that passage or to address the implications of the 5 husbands in John 4 in order to stick to my central subject of holiness).

But both of these occurrences remind us how important it is to preserve our marriages for the sake of Jesus Christ if this is possible. If it proves to be impossible, then we need to recover from the spiritual shock and continue to trust Jesus Christ to provide what and whom we need according to the circumstances of our case. I am convinced that remarriage is permissible at least where an original spouse commits adultery (Matthew 19:1-12) or deserts permanently (1 Corinthians 7:10-17), but that anyone who has a divorce regardless of reason cannot serve as a pastor or deacon based on 1 Timothy 3 and Titus 1. But any person in such a situation should not focus on what he cannot do but rather on what God does want him to do from now forward. To the extent that any person knows that he or she has sinned in any fashion, one must repent and change from the sinful direction or attitude to a more godly one. There are amazing stories, starting with the Apostles, about how much God has accomplished through very imperfect men and women.

We should also remember that God restrains even the sin that we commit and the sin that others commit against us. He will not allow anything that will not be to the ultimate good of the believer and of His people. Romans 8:28 is true in all situations for the believer over the long run. I know of at least one situation where God permitted one party to a marriage to commit adultery in order to amputate that spouse from the other's life. In that case He chose to graft into the place of amputation a much more suitable spouse, to the joy of both in the second marriage. The saying that "two wrongs do not make a right" is certainly true among sinful people. But as it is written, *"The things that are impossible with men are possible with God."* Luke 18:27. We must trust Him through the fog of crisis.

CHAPTER 5

---◠◦◠---

Holiness, Work & Economic Impact

A century ago, it was taken for granted that the rise of Biblical Christianity in Europe had major economic impacts. Today this has been largely forgotten. But the Bible affirms that holiness and prosperity, properly understood, go hand in hand with each other. For example, consider:

> *Honor your father and your mother, as the LORD your God hath commanded you; that your days may be prolonged, and that it may go well with you, in the land which the LORD your God gives you.* Deuteronomy 5:16

> *Hear therefore, O Israel, and observe to do; that it may be well with you, and that you may increase mightily, as the LORD God of thy fathers hath promised you, in the land that flows with milk and honey.* Deuteronomy 6:3

> *Blessed is every one that fears the LORD; that walks in his ways. For you shalt eat the labor of your hands: you shall be happy and it shall be well with you.* Psalm 128:1-2

The Bible does not promise that every believer will be wealthy in the perishable goods or money of this world. Indeed the qualities of a believer generally tend to economic independence and solvency, but we should not assume that the poor lack favor with God, especially if the poor shows the peace of God and the characteristics of holiness. It is quite possible for a widow who put in her last coin into the treasury to have more wealth in heaven than the richest businessperson on earth. Our Lord Jesus owned nothing except His seamless robe and did not even have a home during the years of His ministry. Matthew 8:20, Luke 9:58. The Hebrew believers commendably accepted theft of their goods for the sake of their faith. Hebrews 10:34. So prosperity in its Biblical sense does not always mean material wealth, although that was included in the cases of Abraham and of Job.

But the primary concern in this essay is the branch of truth that shows that national holiness generally is conducive to economic independence and improvement. Israel during the earlier portion of King Solomon's rule up through the visit of the Queen of Sheba is a prime example. In the providence of God I believe that there are two main branches of this:

1. God's direct blessing; (Ezekiel 36:29, Isaiah 35, Joshua 1:8; for the opposite principle Haggai 2:14-18, Malachi 2:2-3) and;
2. God's blessing through natural causation. (Proverbs 10:4 and 21:5 and for the opposite, most of the book of Joel.)

We should take each of these in turn.

One example of the direct blessing of God is the economic recovery of Job after his repentance. *"The Lord gave Job twice as much as he had before."* Job 42:10. In addition, God replaced all 10 of Job's children who had died in the whirlwind. As concerning the nation of Israel at the end, we read in Ezekiel 36:29-30, *"I will save you from all your uncleannesses, and I will call for the corn and will increase it and lay no famine upon you. And I will multiply the fruit of the tree and the increase of the field, that you receive no more reproach of famine from the heathen."* With these passages as examples, we can see that God from time to time intervenes directly to uphold His people economically, although we should also notice in Ezekiel that God cleanses Israel spiritually and morally and then economically. Many years ago I can remember a Friday early in my law practice when at 2:00 PM I did not have the money in my account to pay my secretary. I prayed—what else could I do? God brought in clients for a will and a deed and the money was indeed there on time. I am sure that countless other believers have similar or far more dramatic experiences.

The natural blessing of God through consequences often occurs as a consequence of diligence and hard work. *"He becomes poor who deals with a slack hand, but the hand of the diligent makes rich."* Proverbs 10:4. *"The thoughts of the diligent tend to plenteousness, but of every one that is hasty only to want."* Proverbs 21:5. This is true in many fields; I am sure that any investor with sense can affirm what Proverbs teaches through their own experience. More generally, we read in Joshua 1:8, *"This book of the Law shall not depart out of your mouth; but you shalt meditate in it day and night, that you may observe to do according to all that is written therein: for then you shalt make your way prosperous, and then you shall have good success."* So there is a connection between obedience to God and at least economic provision, if not necessarily great wealth. David's observation near the end of his life is pertinent: *"I have been young and am old, yet I have not seen the righteous forsaken, nor his seed begging bread."* Psalm 37:25.

One way that God may curse a company or an economy is through the consequences of illicit drug usage or drunkenness at or after work. How much work has to be scrapped or redone because of errors made by workers who are under the influence of some substance or are "hung over?" How much financial crime is committed under the influence of some form of stimulant? How many fights are triggered in part by drug usage (for examples, amphetamines and alcohol), with all of the resulting lost time and legal costs even in the absence of physical injury? And how many workers are injured physically because of subtle errors committed because either the injured worker or a co-workers was less than fully alert because of some substance's side effects? How much "road rage" is caused at least in part by prior usage of a drug? One God can quantify this precisely, but at least in the United States the true total cost must be staggering. One of the major drivers of our high cost of medical care is our use of drugs that are intended to blow the mind, not even considering the mental side effects of legal drugs that have some legitimate use but are overused in order to seek a "high." And such use deprives us of the best thinking of the users and often of their family members too.

We must be careful to avoid what is sometimes called "prosperity teaching," which states that if you love God you will quickly become rich in this earthly life. This is not necessarily true. The Apostle Paul testified,

"I know how to be abased and how to abound. Everywhere and in all things I am instructed both to be full and to be hungry, both to abound and to suffer need." Philippians 4:12. Yet it is true that if your desires are conformed to the will of God, your desires will be met and you will experience joy in your life. Other things being equal, inner joy tends to support physical health. Many forms of true riches cannot be deposited in a bank. And remember that there is not a simple correlation between riches and joy; some of the most unhappy people in the world are or at least once were wealthy. Drug abuse and suicide occur among the wealthy as well as among the poor. How happy were Elvis Presley and Michael Jackson when they were taking fatal overdoses? Was Marilyn Monroe happy with all of her wealth and fame? How happy was the Emperor Nero when his own guard was hunting him down? And how happy was Hitler hiding out in his bunker? As the Lord Jesus said in the Sermon on the Mount, *"Lay not up for yourselves treasures on earth, where moth and rust corrupt and thieves break through and steal. But lay up for yourselves treasures in heaven, where moth and rust do not corrupt nor do thieves break through and steal."* Matthew 6:19-20.

As to having enough without the added responsibility and troubles for most people of enormous wealth, consider this prayer from Proverbs 30:8-9:

> *"Remove far from me vanity and lies: give me neither poverty nor riches; feed me with food convenient for me: lest I be full, and deny You, and say, 'Who is the Lord?' or lest I be poor, and steal, and take the name of my God in vain."*

Now we should consider briefly how holiness in living the Christian life should suit a person of suitable age and training to be productive in the economy.

1. A Christian should be trustworthy. For an employer, there are few things worse than an undependable employee. *"He that sends a message by the hand of a fool cuts off the feet and drinks damage."* Proverbs 26:6. The Lord Jesus also told a parable of two sons told to work in their father's fields. One said he would go and did not; the other initially refused but then changed his mind

(repented) and went. Matthew 21:28-30. Certainly it was better to actually go even after refusal than to deceive the father and break a promise.

2. A Christian should be honest. *"Do not lie to one another, seeing that you have put off the old man and his deeds."* Colossians 3:9.

3. A Christian should be sober at all times, both in the sense of avoiding intoxication and in the sense of a sober self-assessment. One never knows when one will get the proverbial phone call at 3:00 in the morning, as Hillary Clinton once phrased it. *"Be sober; be vigilant, for your adversary, the Devil, walks about, seeking whom he may devour."* 1 Peter 5:8. 1 Thessalonians 5:6-8 likewise instructs us to be sober, and there are further references in Titus 2. As to self-assessment, consider Romans 12:3: *"For this I say through the grace given to me, to every man that is among you, that you should not think [of himself] more highly than he ought to think, but to think soberly, according as God has dealt to every man the measure of faith."* The benefits of an honest and sober self-assessment in the world of work are obvious.

4. A Christian should be concentrating on his tasks rather than on outside worries. As the Lord Jesus taught in Matthew 6:34, *"Do not take thought to tomorrow, for tomorrow will take thought for the things of itself. Sufficient for the day is its own troubles."* In avoiding certain forms of obvious sin, the Christian likewise avoids the fear of detection and fear of the consequences of those sins which were never committed in the first place.

5. A Christian should avoid gossip in the office as well as in other places. *"The words of a talebearer are as wounds, and they go down to the innermost parts of the belly."* Proverbs 18:8 repeated in Proverbs 26:22. *"Where there is no wood, the fire goes out. So where there is no talebearer, the strife ceases."* Proverbs 26:20. *"A talebearer reveals secrets, but he that is of a faithful spirit conceals the matter."* Proverbs 11:13. Whether one is dealing with classified information, competitive secrets, office confidences, confidential legal material or simply personal data, a Christian should be of a faithful spirit and preserve the secrets, with rare exceptions such as a plot to commit a future crime.

6. A Christian should avoid disrupting other workers' families. This is an obvious corollary to the Commandments against stealing,

adultery, false witness and coveting anyone or anything belonging to a neighbor. In the work context, this would cover any attempts to seduce someone else's spouse as well as many other sins.

7.   A Christian should be willing to give unwelcome advice when necessary. In 1 Kings 22, Micaiah the prophet warned Kings Jehoshaphat and Ahab that God would not bless their attack against Syria, and that Ahab would be killed. Ahab tried to disguise his identity, but God was not fooled. Micaiah was thrown in jail for a short time on short rations of bread and water for his courage, but Ahab indeed ended up dead from a battle wound within a few days. A sensible employer will afterward appreciate a timely warning even if the warning was disregarded at first.

TRENDS UNFAVORABLE TO CHRISTIANS IN WORK:

A.   Christians as a whole will not look the other way when stealing or false practices occur. Some employers will not like it, and in other cases fellow workers will plot to have the Christian removed from where he or she can see the false practices;

B.   Christians are viewed as dull and lacking creativity. This is not true. Many Christians have contributed tremendously to the welfare of the world. Oliver Cromwell in effect invented the weekend, with the general pattern of 5 days of work, 1 day of work at home, and 1 day of worship and rest. Michael Faraday and Joseph Henry contributed tremendously to our knowledge of electricity. S. Truett Cathay today runs Chick-Fil-A, a business he founded after World War 2. Other businesses with Christian origins were ServPro, Thomas Nelson & Sons, J.C. Penney, Colgate-Palmolive and Integrity Music. Sanderson Farms still has a strong Christian influence;

C.   Christians will not approve wild parties, mind-altering drug usage, office affairs and other similar detrimental conduct;

D.   Christians will refuse to lie when the employer wants them to do so for profit or convenience;

E. Christians are more likely to be concerned about the effect of their work and their hours on their families, if married. This concern is not unique to Christians but it is associated with Christianity. In some fields, people are expected to exchange sexual benefits for favor or information. Christians as a whole will refuse.

TECHNOLOGICAL TRENDS REDUCING EMPLOYMENT AFFECTING CHRISTIAN AND NON-CHRISTIAN ALIKE

1. Highly skilled workers and even geniuses are able to accomplish more by themselves with computers, so that fewer assistants are needed. The same is true with smaller, more closely knit teams. A business team that clicks can do more and earn more proportionately than in earlier eras of weaker technology.

2. The costs of employing a person (such as family leave, insurance, taxes, etc.) are rising, giving more impetus to replacing workers with machines and robots. This first affected unskilled blue-collar jobs involving physical labor that were primarily male, but it is now affecting primarily female retail sales jobs such as self-service checkouts. The trend is toward fewer, more skilled workers extending their reach with computers and robots. The jobs that are created, such as programming, are skilled jobs dissimilar to the unskilled jobs destroyed. More and more phone solicitations are recorded rather than with a live caller.

3. More specialized knowledge is necessary to compete in the economy than used to be the case. Such specialized knowledge commands more pay and often costs more to obtain. There is far less room for generalized intelligence and character that an employer will train for one or more desired purposes. It used to be common for an employer to hire a "keeper" even if the new employee would need some initial training before he or she would pay off. The idea was formerly to get the good prospect started somewhere and then we'll figure out how to make his or her potential pay off. But this is "old school." The new idea is to

expect even a new employee to hit the ground running from the very start.

4. There is less loyalty in the employment marketplace than there used to be, at least in the private sector. This applies both ways; employees feel much more free to leave and employers feel far more free to dismiss rather than attempt retraining or transfer when one job situation is not working as anticipated. One instance of this is the GE practice of Jack Welch to have GE departments fire their lowest 10% or 20% of their employees in their current jobs. Sometimes this is necessary, but there are other instances when the underperforming person is in the wrong place but would blossom in another position. Also, employees are more inclined to serve faithfully where they are while looking for better opportunities within the organization than when they are looking outside. This trend, sometimes amounting to impatience on both sides, fosters instability in labor markets.

5. It is more difficult for older workers to keep pace in many modern workplaces. This makes older workers more liable to be fired and makes it an uphill battle for older workers to get another job when they are fired, even when the firing is clearly without cause. Part of this relates to increased use of social media which is more familiar to younger workers. Hours of work in many industries are far longer than the old standard of 40 hours. Some computer companies schedule all-night brainstorming sessions. This is hard on older workers and especially hard on those with children. Indirectly, this trend is probably adverse to most Christians in such industries because Christians tend to be more family-oriented than the workforce as a whole, but that does not mean that such policies are deliberately intended to discriminate based on religion. There are many instances in which both men and women report that the fact that they are raising families places them at a disadvantage in employment.

In making such points, we should not oversell how far sound personal or national economics can make our lives better. *"And Jesus looked all around and said to His disciples, 'How hardly shall they that have riches enter the Kingdom of God!' And the disciples were astonished at His words. But Jesus answered again and said to them, 'Children, how hard it is for those who trust in riches to enter the Kingdom of God.'"* Mark 10:23-24. There is no intrinsic virtue of poverty unless it is a necessary condition for a particular work for God to which a particular person is called, but both poverty and riches present temptations for the soul to be preoccupied with our present life on this earth. Our primary concern must be with our future in heaven with secondary concern for necessary matters now. What this means in practical terms will vary from person to person.

It is also true that sound economic policy will not always benefit a nation, especially one who culture and purposes are against those of God. God can and does frustrate shrewd counsel for an evil cause as he frustrated Ahithophel's shrewd counsel to Absalom in 2 Samuel 17. The blessings of good economic policies may be lost totally because of spiritual evil in a nation. From what we know, Sodom did not suffer from bad economic policy but from spiritual wickedness that expressed itself in both same-sex and opposite-sex abhorrent practices, leading to judgment. As one can see in Revelation, there is no economic defense against the judgments of God.

CHAPTER 6

—◦◦◦—

Acrostic of Jesus Christ Pertaining to Holiness:

A One aspect of the holiness of Jesus Christ is that He is the <u>Alpha</u> and the Omega (Revelation 1:8) and likewise the <u>Author</u> and Finisher of faith (Hebrews 12:2). Thus He has started us down the road of faith to make us part of the people for His own possession (1 Peter 2:9). He has saved us by grace through faith (and He is the Author of faith, and our faith originates in Him and not in ourselves—Ephesians 2:8) in order to start to make us holy and fit for His presence forever.

B Jesus Christ is the <u>Bridegroom</u> of the holiest and last marriage ever to occur, between Jesus Christ and His Church as the Bride. Revelation 19:8-9 and much of Revelation 21 & 22. He gave His physical life and body in order to redeem the Bride from her sins and to purify her.

C Jesus Christ sends the <u>Comforter</u> (John 16:7). Since the Comforter is the Holy Spirit (John 14:26), the Lord Jesus is sending the Spirit so that we should be holy in obedience to the ancient Scripture, *"I am the Lord Who brings you up out of the land of Egypt, to be your God. You shall be holy for I am holy,' says the Lord."* Leviticus 11:44-5. We are set free from the power of sin as the ancient Israelites were set free from the power of Pharaoh. We exchange a wicked, sinful and cruel master for a holy and loving Master, Jesus Christ. *"Come to Me, all you who labor and are heavily burdened. Take My yoke upon you and learn from Me, for I am meek and lowly of heart, and you shall find rest for your souls. For My yoke is easy and My burden is light."* Matthew 11:28-30.

D The Lord Jesus is a <u>divider</u> between the faithful and the unfaithful, between the righteous and the unrighteous, between the true and the false. He warns in Luke 12:51, *"Do you suppose that I am come to give peace on earth? I tell you 'no,' but rather, division."* As recorded in John 7:43, 9:16 and 10:19, Jesus Christ in fact caused division among His contemporaries. In Matthew 25:32, starting His account of the Last Judgment, the Lord Jesus starts off dividing the sheep from the goats. So once again Jesus Christ will act as a divider. How can this be when He is the Prince of Peace (Isaiah 9:6)? The answer is that there is only peace among the holy saints of God; there is no peace between the converted and saved saints of God and the adherents of Satan. They must be divided first and the wicked must be judged before there will be a final peace. There may be a temporary peace or truce between a Christian and his or her unbelieving neighbors (Proverbs 16:7), but this does not endure because Satan himself never lets up in his hatred for the Lord Jesus. Sooner or later the war will break out anew until the end. This is why the Apostle Paul speaks of armor in Ephesians 6:10-18. So the Biblical order expressed in Revelation is that Jesus Christ will fight and win the Battle of Armageddon first and then use that victory to impose His peace.

E Jesus Christ is <u>essential</u> to everything that is good and holy. As to physics, it is He Who exerts the force of gravity. *"By Him all things hold together."* Colossians 1:17. As imperfect as human governments are, it is Christ Who keeps everything from falling into political disorder and anarchy, just as He by gravity prevents the earth from disintegrating. *"For by Him were all things created, that are in heaven and that are in earth, visible and invisible, whether thrones, dominions, principalities or powers. All things were created by Him and for Him."* Colossians 1:16. Yes, Satan marred the original perfect Creation after his own fall into pride and total sin, and Jesus Christ is now preserving that in its fallen condition until the time of its removal and preparing to fight total warfare against sin in order to undo and destroy all that Satan has done (Hebrews 2:14, 1 John 3:8). The Book of Revelation makes it graphically clear that the warfare will focus on earth but will also have effects throughout the heavens as well. The final warfare will be short and sharp beyond any human experience to date, even counting World War 2. But in the end Jesus Christ will be triumphant and will crush all of His enemies into the dust and then into the fire forever.

In the meantime the Lord Jesus and His Father control our breath (Job 12:9-10, 34:13-15; Psalm 104:29; Isaiah 42:5), our food (Matthew 6:11) and everything else we need to be sustained until it is His time to take us home to heaven.

F Jesus Christ is a glorious <u>Friend</u> and capable when provoked of great <u>fury</u>. This paradox at first is hard to understand, but both qualities can readily be verified from the Bible. On earth, someone who has been involved in combat knows that a good soldier is capable of great tenderness towards a wounded comrade and great fury directed to the enemy. A gentle husband may turn into a tiger if someone threatens his wife. If these things are true of sinful human beings, how much more would they apply to the Lord Jesus, the perfect Son of Man?

Consider the friendship of Jesus Christ towards His disciples, most especially toward John and even toward Judas, whom the Lord Jesus knew to be the traitor. Matthew 26:50. Abraham was called the *"friend of God."* James 2:23. As the Lord Jesus said shortly before His death in John 15:13-15, *"Greater love has no man than this, that a man should lay down his life for his friends. You are My friends if you do whatsoever I command you. From now on I do not call you servants, for a servant does not know what his Lord does. But I have called you friends, because all things that I have heard from My Father I have made known to you."* Moses and Elijah had especially close encounters with the Father, and our Friend the Lord Jesus is seated at His Father's right hand. Hebrews 1:3.

Taking the other side of the coin, consider this verse from Nahum 1:2 *"God is jealous, and the Lord takes revenge. The Lord takes revenge and is furious. The Lord will take vengeance on His adversaries and He reserves wrath for His enemies."* Again He says, *"Vengeance is Mine; I will repay."* Romans 12:19, see also Isaiah 59:18. Revelation 6, 8-9, 14, 16 and 19 portray the wrath of Jesus Christ upon a defiant world. The vast scope of the vengeance is shown by the concentration of carrion birds at the end of Revelation 19. We should also remember that His fury at His enemies is connected with His friendship for His people and His anger at abuse directed at His people. Luke 18:7-8, Revelation 6:10.

G The Lord is <u>gracious.</u> Joel 2:13 says in part, *"Rend your hearts and not your garments, and turn to the Lord your God. For He is gracious and merciful, slow to anger and of great kindness . . ."* I might try to paraphrase the next part of the verse like this: "He readily holds back from inflicting disaster." Jonah learned that to be true. But we should not presume that God will hold back forever. Judgment will fall with unstoppable force, and humanity is declining morally to the point where it may reasonably be expected soon. But we cannot now say just when the judgment will fall.

We have already observed the saving grace of the Lord Jesus, putting His own body on the line to save us when we were offensive to Him and were His natural enemies. Romans 5:8. But His grace continues after the atonement to cleansing grace as we walk through life. That is what the foot-washing symbolizes in John 13:4-16. The grace of the Lord Jesus extends from initial salvation all the way to everlasting life in heaven.

The Lord Jesus is also <u>gentle</u> with His people. After Peter denied Him because of his opposition to the Cross, Peter tried to quit his apostleship to go back to fishing. As related in John 21, the Lord Jesus concealed himself as a mere bystander at the lake when Peter and some other disciples had taken no fish all night. Then the Lord brought Peter a tremendous catch as a farewell to fishing. He even retained Peter in his place as first among equals among the apostles.

In John 8 the Lord Jesus was also very gentle with the woman caught in adultery and dragged before Him for judgment. We do not know what He wrote on the ground, but whatever it was drove all the witnesses away. Since there were no witnesses, He let the woman go free in accord with the Law of Moses. We observe that principle even today that witnesses must prove a crime. He did warn her to sin no more, but our Lord Jesus treated her very gently. One could likewise see His gentleness with the hardened woman at the well in John 4. He did confront her with her sin of cohabitation without benefit of marriage, but not harshly. He gently led her to the real issue of whom should be worshiped and saved her soul. A third instance of gentleness is His permitting John to lean against His chest at the Last Supper (John 13:25).

H Jesus Christ is <u>honorable.</u> He has never made a promise that He has not kept. For example, let us take the promise of the Great Commission, *"All authority is given to Me in heaven and in earth. . . . And I will be with you always, even to the end of the age."* Matthew 28:18, 20. With a working knowledge of history, we can see how the Lord Jesus has kept His promise. None of us can know the exact number of those who have laid down their lives for the testimony of Jesus Christ. We do know that they span time, culture, language, ethnic origin and every other human characteristic one can name. Were there martyrs in Stalinist Russia? Probably there were millions. What about Maoist China? There were millions there too. Going back to the days of the Roman Empire takes us to the Apostles Peter and Paul and to unnumbered other martyrs, both in Rome and in the provinces. Are there English martyrs? Yes, about 2 per week in the days of Queen Mary, daughter of Henry VIII. Representing Central Europe would be Jan Hus and Jerome of Prague in the early 1400s. It is said that Jerome sang from the Psalms as he was being burned to death. The Apostle Thomas was the first of many to die for the Master in India. And there are martyrs recorded in 20th century South America in jungle areas that we are prone to consider primitive (true, they lack electricity upon which we rely but they also have resources that we hardly comprehend at all). In France? One can start with Admiral de Coligny in 1572. Or first-century Israel? There are Stephen, one of the original seven deacons, and James, half-brother of the Lord Jesus Christ. In America? Yes, Cassie Bernal at Columbine was killed upon a brief profession of her faith. One could go on, as the writer of Hebrews intimated in Hebrews 11:32-40. Only God can count the martyrs' deaths that occurred outside the reach of recorded history. But the millions of deaths in faith under extreme pressure should be persuasive that Jesus Christ has kept His promise through all time and all cultures.

The Lord Jesus keeps His promises. Take another example: *"Come to Me, all you who labor and are heavily burdened, and I will give you rest. Take My yoke upon you and learn from Me, for I am meek and lowly of heart, and you shall find rest for your souls."* Matthew 11:28-29. Countless Christians from every walk of life and every portion of the globe will testify how the Lord Jesus has kept this promise in their lives. They may be of exceptionally powerful emotions like Martin Luther or strongly intellectual like C.S. Lewis, to pick but two people of greatly contrasting temperaments. But both have testified of the peace of God even in extreme stress when in their lives they were driven to the wall.

Jesus Christ is also <u>honorable</u> in another sense, in that He has paid all the debt for sin of His entire family. He undertakes to provide for His own even though we are not intrinsically worthy of His preservation. He assumed and paid in full our debt and penalty for sin and now is delivering His people from a deserved death. Instead of repudiating the debt incurred by His chosen people, He paid and honored it. In so doing He went beyond the requirements of the Law.

I Jesus Christ is <u>inclusive</u> in two senses: He has taken as His own people of every conceivable ethnic background and combination and He has taken for His own diverse people with almost every possible variety of sin in their background. Virtually all classes and occupations can be found. By the time of the end, every language group and nationality will be present among His assembled people. "Go and teach all nations . . ." Matthew 28:19. In response, there will be people in heaven from *"every kindred, tongue, people and nation . . ."* Revelation 5:9.

However, Jesus Christ excludes those who cling to their sin instead of giving it up. *"Don't you know that the unrighteous will not inherit the kingdom of God? Do not be deceived. Neither fornicators, nor idolaters, nor effeminate, nor abusers of themselves with mankind, nor thieves, nor covetous, nor drunkards, nor revilers, nor extortioners shall inherit the kingdom of God."* I Corinthians 6:9-10. And then Paul adds, *"And such were some of you, but you are washed . . ."* See also Revelation 22:14-15: *"Blessed are they that do His commandments, that they may have the right to the Tree of Life, and enter through the gates into the city. For outside are dogs and sorcerers and whoremongers and murderers and idolaters and whoever loves and makes a lie."* Holiness is necessary to enter the city even though it is not the means of initial entry into the city. We cannot come by faith because we are not naturally holy. Rather, we come by grace through faith, and then the holiness grows until we reach perfection. But the unholy are excluded and punished forever.

J Jesus Christ will be a <u>just judge.</u> See Matthew 25:31-46. He will have all the facts. He will know the exact thoughts and motives of everyone. No hidden influences or accomplices will escape His notice. For so many, that's precisely the problem—concealment from Him is impossible. And if we consult our consciences, we all know that we have thoughts and actions that we would prefer to hide. We all know we have sinned. What is the solution? To confess now what you can't hide in any case and ask forgiveness now on the basis of Jesus' death at the Cross and His Resurrection as the Lord of Glory. If you repent and are forgiven now you won't be judged for eternity later, but rather forgiven forever.

K In human government, we dare not follow the old Roman pattern and have the Emperor judge cases as well as carry out the law. That involves too much power, too much responsibility and too much strain on one individual. Even Moses had to delegate the hearing of routine legal cases to trained judges. Exodus 18:13-27. But what is necessary for fallible human beings is contrary to the glory of the Lord Jesus Christ.

When Jesus Christ reigns as <u>King of Kings</u>, He will have all power in His hands. 1 Timothy 6:15. As Judge, He will sentence or forgive every individual who has ever been conceived, even those who have never been born. God used Moses as a lawgiver; the Lord Jesus is Himself the ultimate authority of the Law of God. He has now and will retain complete control over all natural elements and phenomena, both in the current world and in the universe to come. Even in the Lake of Fire, Jesus Christ is the Ruler carrying out His eternal sentences and decrees—Satan is the arch-prisoner and greatest sufferer, not a jail warden like the one whom the ancient Joseph assisted. Remember that *"at the name of Jesus every knee [shall] bow . . . and every tongue [shall] confess Jesus as Lord, to the glory of God the Father . . ."* Philippians 2:10-11.

L To the extent that there may be a distinction between kingship and <u>lordship</u>, it may be that lordship is more personal than kingship. For most of us, our connection with the President of the United States, the King of Thailand, or whomever might be the national leader is impersonal. With our boss at work or our teacher at school, it's personal. When the Lord Jesus destroyed the skepticism of the Apostle Thomas, he confessed Jesus as *"My Lord and my God."* John 20:28. For Thomas it was personal; he knew the Lord Jesus personally and the Lord knew Thomas. The Lord Jesus exercises direct personal and intimate supervision over us in addition to His crown rights as King.

M The Lord Jesus is also our <u>Master</u> in addition to being our King and our Lord. We are therefore His slaves, as Paul says of himself in the introductions of numerous epistles. This is true in terms of the absolute power of the Lord Jesus over us, but in fact in His generosity He often treats us as friends or even children when He retains the right to treat us as slaves or as soldiers under His direct command. But the term "Master" has another dimension: He is a master craftsman (for example, Genesis 1:26 and Proverbs 8:30) and we are His apprentices, yoked with Him for training (Matthew 11:28-30, 1 Corinthians 3:9) and instruction. God has not saved us for mere drudgery, although some of the service required may be very humbling as in the case of our Lord washing the disciples' feet (even the feet of the traitor Judas!) in John 13:4-12. He has saved us to pool our labor, whether physical or intellectual or both, like a jigsaw puzzle to create a beautiful portrait of Christlike love for display to the world. All of our service supplies some portion of the entire portrait, and none of us can even come close to supplying all or even most of the picture. Paul uses the metaphor of the human body in 1 Corinthians 12:14-31 to make the same basic point. Christ is the Head (Ephesians 5:23), and we as parts of the body obey the Head.

N Jesus Christ is the Ruler of all <u>nature,</u> as Bernard of Clairvaux declared in the old hymn "Fairest Lord Jesus." He controls the wind and the waves (for example, Matthew 14:22-33) and was even in His human body able to walk on water and lift Peter while walking on water. The eyewitnesses in the boat were persuaded, at least for the moment and eventually permanently, that He is the Son of God. In a similar vein, our Lord Jesus stated that His Father knew the whereabouts of every sparrow in the world. (Matthew 10:29-31, Luke 12:6-7). Indeed God know not only about every living thing, but even about every living cell within every living thing. The Lord Jesus used the example that the hairs on our heads are all numbered. In my case that would be less of a task than for many, so let me use another example which is part of how God supplies our daily needs.

We all need healthy bacteria in our digestive tracts in order to digest our food well. For God it is not simply a matter of supplying our food; He also supplies the invisible microbes that help us digest it well and with minimal pain. One way He does this is to have created cows and necessary bacteria long ago in order to make yogurt possible. Yogurt is good for most people because it replenishes the invisible good bacteria which are our allies in daily living.

As a brief aside, this interdependency among contrasting species is one reason why random evolution is preposterous. Did the bacteria survive without their human hosts, or with no animal hosts at all? If so, what and how did they eat? But if not, then these beneficial bacteria and human beings must have come to life at the same time and found each other. Is that random? Hardly! Or as the French would say aptly,

<<*Mille fois non!*>>—a thousand times no! Evolution is important in the history of ideas, and people seeking to prove evolution have made useful discoveries in the same way that medieval alchemists made useful discoveries in the course of their efforts to turn other metals into gold. But when weighed as truth, random macro-evolution is a modern myth. The Father, Son and Spirit worked together on Creation as Moses through the Holy Spirit declared in Genesis 1 & 2 and as Solomon explained in Proverbs 8. Also, one can start with Job 38 and read through the end of that book for one illustration of how important God considers Creation.

Viewed another way, God's knowledge of each living cell can be conceived of as a vast network. As to the information facet, one can conceptualize the Father, Son and Holy Spirit as a incomparable computer network of three enormous super-computers which instantaneously mirror each other as data changes cell by cell, atom by atom and electron by electron and down to any smaller particles that may exist. No computer network designed by sinful people will ever come close to this. My computer network analogy does not come close to portraying God in His fulness. Remember that each member of the Trinity is a full person. They have not only information, intelligence and memory, but also emotions and all attributes of a human being. Before the sin of Adam and Eve, as human beings we were modeled after God. Even after the Fall, we have fragmented portions of the divine attributes that we had originally. One day every believer will regain all that was lost in the Fall, and more besides. But for the contemporary generation the most comprehensible explanation I can give for the vast knowledge and power of God is a super-computer network.

O The computer network example that we just used should help us understand that God is omniscient, omnipresent, and omnipotent. It took such a powerful God to create our ecosystem. The Greek prefix "omni" means "all" with respect to whatever attribute "omni" may be attached. I can say all of these words about God, but that does not mean that I understand this fully. I don't. I would recommend strongly a study on Psalm 139 for a greater appreciation of the vastness of God and the comparative puniness of humanity. See Isaiah 40:15 for another example.

P The Lord Jesus is <u>precious,</u> as Peter states in 1 Peter 2:7. And this is true notwithstanding the fact that the majority rejects Him most of the time, whether in 1ˢᵗ-century Jerusalem, 21ˢᵗ-century America, or other countries for most or all of their history. During the years leading to the Tribulation and during the Tribulation itself, that rejection will grow, as we already observe as I write at the end of 2013. He is precious because He gave His life to save His sheep, as stated most directly in John 10:11 but also in Matthew 20:28, Romans 5:6-8, Titus 2:14, Hebrews 9:28 and 1 Peter 2:24-25.

Even before He had endured the Cross, a very few women understood His preciousness. In 1ˢᵗ-century Israel, it is unlikely that they had had theological training. Their understanding must have come through revelation by the Holy Spirit to them, perhaps through their intuition first rather than their rational minds. Luke 7:36-50; Matthew 26:1-13 (and the corresponding accounts in Mark 14:3-9 and John 12:3-8). To them, and also to the women who took the spices to Jesus' tomb on the day of His resurrection, He was precious and worth the most expensive spices and ointments that could be procured. In fact, this realization by a few brackets the life of our Lord Jesus. Shortly after He was born, the *magii* carried precious ointments and spices along with gold to worship Him. Simeon and Anna recognized Him as Messiah as Joseph and Mary brought Him to the Temple to be dedicated. But at the time of His birth as well as His death, the authorities hated Him to the point of wanting Him dead. The *magii* were warned in a dream not to return to Herod because of his murderous intent. Directed by a dream from God, Joseph and Mary fled to Egypt ahead of Herod's murderous soldiers who slaughtered the male children. But when His time to give His life had come, the Lord Jesus walked straight to Jerusalem, the city spiritually called Sodom and Egypt (Revelation 11:8). Yet in the end the Lord Jesus will deliver Jerusalem not merely from domination by Gentile powers but from domination by Satan in the realm of worship and ideas. As passages like Isaiah 2, 11 and 60 prophesy, Jerusalem will eventually become the purest city yet seen on earth through Jesus the Messiah. Yes, He is precious.

Q Jesus Christ will give no <u>quarter</u> to Satan nor to sin at the Last Judgment. The time when quarter is possible for living human beings ends with physical death. *"It is appointed to men once to die, and after* *this the Judgment."* Hebrews 9:27. As Matthew 25:31-46 makes plain, there are no gray areas there. By analogy, in older warfare such as during the English Civil War it was understood that some mercy would be shown to the survivors of a surrendering city or fortress if it surrendered immediately after a breach was made in the walls. But if surrender was still refused, no further opportunity for quarter could be expected. Psychologically, this could be understood because of the fury aroused in storming the fortress and in the killing that would accompany a storm. A somewhat similar situation existed between the United States and Japan when Japan would not surrender before the two atom bombs were dropped. In today's society, in some arrest or hostage situations there is no further opportunity for a defendant to surrender alive without gunfire if he refuses to come out with his hands up when surrounded. Right now, quarter and everlasting mercy are offered to any person who will repent and surrender to Jesus Christ. But that window is closing rapidly. *"Behold, now is the accepted time. Now is the day of salvation."* 2 Corinthians 6:2.

R Jesus Christ is the first of a multitude of saints to be <u>resurrected.</u> *"I am the Resurrection and the Life. He who believes on Me, though he were dead, yet shall he live."* John 11:25. For the Christian, the death of this body is almost like a snake shedding its skin. Our temporary tabernacle (2 Peter 1:14) is left behind and we receive a glorious new body like the new body of our Lord Jesus Christ (Philippians 3:21, also see 1 Corinthians 15 for an extended treatment of the bodily resurrection). Unlike the snake in nature, we become a completely purified soul as well as receiving a new body. Resurrection also can be compared to metamorphosis of a caterpillar into a butterfly, where an ugly caterpillar which appears to be buried completely in its cocoon becomes a complete new and beautiful creature (although still mortal, unlike the immortality of the resurrected Christian). Every believer will be resurrected or raptured to everlasting life with full union with Jesus Christ.

S Jesus Christ is the <u>Savior</u> of all of His people. His offer of salvation shall be proclaimed universally, to all people of every language and every descent. From what are His people saved? When considered from an eternal standpoint, His people are saved from their deserved judgment and wrath at the hand of Almighty God. Considered from the standpoint of our remaining life on earth, the Lord Jesus saves His people from the domination of sin over their lives and starts the process of their perfection. Before salvation, people are dead in their spirits as a consequence of Adam's spiritual death (as distinct from his physical death centuries later) when he disobeyed God and ate the forbidden fruit. But when Christ enters our life, our spirits are likewise made alive. Unlike our bodies, our spirits will never die again. As our Lord Jesus said to Martha, *"Whosoever believes on Me will never die. Do you believe this?"* John 11:26. I repeat the Lord's question to Martha: Do you believe this?

T The Lord Jesus will be <u>triumphant.</u> We usually think of triumph and victory as practically the same thing. In considering the Roman context, a triumph was a parade in Rome awarded to a Roman general victorious in a major campaign. Not every victorious commander was awarded a public triumph. The Apostle Paul understood the distinction and used the word "triumph" concerning the Lord Jesus in Colossians 2:15, *"Having spoiled principalities and powers, He made a show of them publicly, triumphing over them in it."* In context, "it" is the Cross. So Satan and his demons were treated like captured prisoners of war before their dispatch into slavery or death at the Cross and the Resurrection. With the Atonement complete, Satan can never gain the loyalty of the entire human race, nor can he divide the Son from the Father as he attempted during the Temptation (Matthew 4:1-11, Luke 4:1-13) or through Peter's initial rejection of the Cross recorded in Matthew 16:21-23. Satan's position in his war against God is totally hopeless. The victory parade of Jesus Christ has already started, and we are permitted to participate behind Him. *"Now thanks be to God, Who always causes us to triumph in Christ, and makes manifest the savor of His knowledge by us in every place."* 2 Corinthians 2:14. So by our lives we can spread the sweet smell of Christ's victory in our particular worlds and participate in His victory parade.

U Jesus Christ is a <u>universal</u> savior. In old translations from Greek confessions the word "catholic" was used in its old sense of universal or of encompassing all cultures. In modern English the word "catholic" has lost that old meaning, so I am using the modern term "universal" to convey this Biblical truth stated in the Great Commission: *"Go and teach all nations, baptizing them in the name of the Father, of the Son and of the Holy Spirit . . ."* Matthew 28:19. Revelation 14:6 gives the ultimate result: *"And I saw another angel fly in the midst of heaven, having the everlasting gospel to* *preach to them who dwell on the earth, to every nation, kindred tongue and people . . ."* And Mark 13:27 tells us that at the very end of days that the elect will come from the most distant parts of the earth as well as from every portion of heaven. It is not true that every person will be saved, but from every race, nationality and language there will be some saved, and all on the equal basis of the blood sacrifice of Jesus Christ for sin at the Cross.

V Jesus Christ is <u>victorious</u> over all of His enemies. If His triumph stresses the parade that comes after the battle, His victory focuses on the battle itself. Isaiah 9 is one passage that makes clear that the victory of the Son of God (note Isaiah 9:6 is in this context) will not be peaceful but will be the result of warfare. Several passages in Revelation (Revelation 6:15-17; Revelation 14, especially 14:10-11, Revelation 17:14; Revelation 19:11-21) also graphically portray the final war which Jesus Christ will win. He will destroy the Devil himself and all his works. Hebrews 2:14; 1 John 3:8. We humans must also beware because Jesus Christ will destroy all of the followers of the Devil as well. And yet believers can rejoice because sin will finally be abolished forever.

W It follows from Jesus' triumph and victory that He is an almighty <u>warrior</u>. And what are His weapons? One weapon is the righteous character of the Lord Jesus. *"And I saw heaven opened, and behold a white horse, and He that sat upon him is called Faithful and True, and in righteousness He does judge and make war."* Revelation 19:11. Another weapon is the Word of God out of the mouth of the resurrected Lord Jesus. The Scriptures in Revelation 19:12-15 continue: *"His eyes are as a flame of fire, and on His head are many crowns, and He had a name that no one knew but He Himself. And He is clothed with clothing dipped with blood, and His name is called the Word of God. And the armies in heaven followed Him on white horses clothed in fine linen, white and clean. And out of His mouth goes a sharp sword, that with it He should strike the nations. And He shall rule them with a rod of iron, and He treads the fierceness of the wrath of Almighty God."*

The Sword going out of the mouth of the Lord Jesus no doubt symbolizes the Word of God, as in Ephesians 6:17. The contrast between the blood-stained clothing of the Lord Jesus and the white and clean linen of His followers shows that He does all the fighting; He alone is dressed for battle, and that battle is swift and short, over in an instant as He speaks from His mouth. His followers are dressed in white linen for the wedding of the Lamb, not for the battle just before.

When our Lord Jesus walked the earth in His human body like ours, He must have used the same weapons as Paul described in Ephesians 6:11-18. This was not because all of this was necessary for Him, but because He was instructing us by demonstrating to us who would follow Him the use of spiritual armor. Starting with verse 12, we know from Matthew 4 and Luke 4 that our Lord Jesus faced the Devil eyeball to eyeball. He met each temptation with a quotation from Deuteronomy and repulsed Satan and his attack. Going to the specific pieces of armor that start in verse 14, the Lord Jesus is the Way, the Truth and the Life, corresponding to the element of truth. We have already covered the fact that the Lord Jesus was sinless (Hebrews 4:15, 7:26).

In Ephesians 6:15, we see the element of the Gospel. The Lord Jesus preached this constantly. His faith was perfect and absolute. He quenched Satan's darts in personal combat. As the Savior, He personified salvation. As we have already notes, the Sword of the Spirit is the Word of God. The final element is prayer. He composed what we call the Lord's Prayer and prayed the High Priestly prayer in John 17 when He was about to be arrested. Luke 6:12 records an instance when the Lord Jesus prayed all night. In Matthew 14:23 we know that He prayed late into the night. So we know that our Lord was and remains the absolute master of spiritual warfare whom we should imitate as far as the Holy Spirit gives us strength, although we will never on earth get close to His endurance or proficiency.

X When the Lord Jesus lived as the Son of Man in His human body that he received from the Virgin Mary, He <u>excelled</u> in all things. An arrest squad came back empty-handed, testifying that *"No man ever spoke like this man."* John 7:46. No other person ever walked on water. Even as a child about 12 years old He was able to hold His own with the greatest rabbis of the day in the Temple. Luke 2:46-47. No other person had ever raised three people from the dead. He healed more people than anyone can count. His healings included the most intractable cases, including people blind, deaf and lame people from birth and people with leprosy. The verdict of the execution squad at the Cross sums it up. The centurion (roughly a 1st Lieutenant, commanding 100 men) spoke for them all, *"Surely this was the Son of God."* Matthew 27:54.

While the Lord Jesus came from heaven instead of from earth (for example, John 6:51), as the Son of Man He compressed His deity into a human body to live and die as a human. For example, He felt weariness (John 4:6 and most of all on the way from His last trial before Pilate to Golgotha, when He could not carry his cross-bar all the way). Almost never did He display His glory as He did on the Mount of Transfiguration. His miracles were profuse by the standards of any other human being but still rare. Most of the time the Lord Jesus subjected Himself to the laws of physics which He had helped set up with His Father during Creation. He even paid taxes as an example to us. So as the Son of Man He was the perfect human being notwithstanding that He was simultaneously the Son of God from heaven.

Y Jesus Christ is a person Who often answers "Yes" to the prayers of His people. The Apostle John has written that *"And this is the confidence that we have in Him, that if we ask anything according to His will, He hears us."* 1 John 5:14. The Lord Jesus laid down the principle at multiple times that God will answer our prayers in His name favorably. Matthew 7:7-11; 18:19; 21:22; Luke 11:9-13; John 14:13-14, 15:7, 16:23-24. We cannot order God around in our prayers and He reserves the right to refuse our requests for our own good and for the good of His kingdom, but if we seek to conform to His holiness (Psalm 66:18) we will not receive refusals from our Father as a matter of routine. If we are afraid to approach Him, we need to re-examine our standing with Him to see why we might be afraid of our Father. There is a sense in which the fear of God is a good thing given how awesome He is and how puny we are, but our faith and intimacy with God must exist in balance with a healthy fear of God. *"Seeing then that we have a great High Priest that has passed into the heavens, Jesus the Son of God, let us hold fast our profession. For we do not have a High Priest that cannot be touched with the feeling of our infirmities, but was in all points tempted as we are, without sin. Let us come boldly before the throne of grace, that we may obtain mercy and find grace to help in time of need."* Hebrews 4:14-16.

Z The Lord Jesus is king in Zion. Psalm 2:6. Hebrews 12:22 tells us that we have come to Mount Zion in contrast to Mount Sinai, the mountain of the Law. Galatians 4:24 starts a similar contrast between Mount Sinai as the Law and the heavenly Jerusalem as the place of freedom, which is often called Zion (or in some versions spelled Sion). Zion is the place of salvation whether referring to Israel on this earth or by extension to the new Jerusalem in heaven. For example, see Psalm 9:11-14, 74:2; Isaiah 12:6, 24:23, 28:16; Isaiah 33, 51. Where we believers are headed, the Lord Jesus already reigns. So we press on eagerly in holiness in preparation to join our Lord in the heavenly Zion.

CHAPTER 7

Sermons and Meditations on Holiness, Fire & Love

FAIR WARNING!

"And these shall go away into everlasting punishment, but the righteous into life eternal." Jesus Christ speaking of the Last Judgment in Matthew 25:46.

Let me start with a story set in 21st century America. In places like California and Colorado, there are mountain valleys and canyons full of wonderful residences with fantastic views. Malibu Canyon is one famous example. Imagine yourself owning one of these mansions surrounded by a forest with a winding road snaking through the canyon to permit road access to the amenities of the big city when you want them. There you are, asleep at 4:00 AM in the middle of a wonderful dream when you hear a pounding on the front door. You sit up in bed and hear a male voice saying, "Get out of here!" Hurry up!"

As you sit up, suppose you respond, "What for? It's the middle of the night. Go away!" That might be reasonable if the folks at the door are impostors and thieves. But in fact the peril is real.

"The canyon's on fire," they reply. "Get out of here while you can." In fact I see embers falling and one corner of your roof may be smoldering."

Then you say, "It's four in the morning. I need to sleep."

Then they respond, "We have no more time to argue with you. We're going to the next house. You have had fair warning."

Indeed you fall back asleep and wake up an hour later to a roaring sound. A hot wind is blowing into the house, and you find yourself coughing from smoke and a burning sensation in your lungs and throat that won't stop. As you roll out of bed, one exterior wall caves in and the ridgepole collapses and traps your legs so that you can no longer move. The fire roars through the house and your pain from both the smoke and the heat intensifies beyond belief. Then the floor of your bedroom catches fire where you are trapped and you are enveloped in flame. It makes no difference whether the flame or the smoke kills your first. Your body is dead and you are now facing a Last Judgment with Jesus Christ as your Judge.

You don't know Him and know very little about Him. The little that you do know terrifies you because you dimly remember that He claimed to be the Son of God and up to your death you did not believe Him. You find that the old saying that there is nothing like a threatened hanging to focus the mind is true, but it's now too late for any of that to do you any good.

I am sure that very few if any of you would be foolish enough to ignore a warning in the middle of the night that a fire is rolling into your neighborhood and that you have to evacuate. Our fictional homeowner ignores reality and ends up dead. There is at least one American counterpart, whose name was Harry R. Truman, not to be confused with the former President Harry S Truman. Both men shared at least two things besides a last name: they served during World War 1 and they both were stubborn. But I will be speaking of the Harry R. Truman who lived near the foot of Mt. Saint Helens, the famous volcano in Washington state. Harry R. Truman was warned repeatedly that he should evacuate his home because of the danger of an eruption. When the eruption took place, Truman's home was buried in about 150 feet of volcanic mud and ash. A destroyed lake may have washed away the home first. We do not know the precise cause of death of Harry R. Truman, but we know that he was blasted to kingdom come by the volcano. And we know that he disregarded repeated warnings to leave while he could.

With all respect I must say that many of you and your friends are more stubborn and more foolish than Mr. Truman. Your house is built on earth. The entire planet is already targeted for a sweeping fire during the Last Days. As the Bible says in 2 Peter 3:7, *"But the heavens and the earth, which are now by the same word reserved to fire against the day of judgment and perdition of ungodly men . . ."* So we all live on ground as dangerous as Mt. Saint Helens, earmarked for judgment and destruction by Almighty God. And we react just as did Mr. Truman and my imaginary homeowner. We want to stay where we are and enjoy what we are now doing, even though God declares so much of our activity sinful.

Viewed from another angle, we identify ourselves as citizens of a country on earth, such as the United States of America, Russia, Thailand, China, Brazil, India, Italy or wherever. This is a temporary necessity because any one-world ruler except for Jesus Christ will be a horror. We cannot have anarchy on the one hand nor any worldwide political power on the other. But every country on earth will one day be destroyed. As the Bible says in Revelation 11:15, *"The kingdoms of this world are become the kingdoms of our Lord and of His Christ, and He shall reign for ever and ever."* Along with the heavenly kingdom to come is a heavenly citizenship: *"For our citizenship is in heaven . . ."* Philippians 3:20. The major portion of our investments likewise should be in heaven, as the Lord Jesus said in the Sermon on the Mount. *"Lay up for yourselves treasures in heaven, where moth and rust do not corrupt nor do thieves break through and steal. For where your treasure is your heart will be also."* Matthew 6:20-21. Because everything on this earth will be destroyed God has prepared for His people a complete new heaven, new earth, new provision and new citizenship.

But before we have all these new things we must first have a new heart. We cannot earn that or do that for ourselves. But we must recognize and admit the necessity of the new heart because of the hardness of the heart that we now have. We all are hardhearted people, offensive to God. In fact the Greek word that the Lord Jesus uses for our hardened hearts when discussing divorce in Matthew 19 is *kardiosclerosis,* which is a compound of Greek medical roots that we still use in English: *kardio* for heart and *sclerosis* for stiffness or hardness, as our arteries tend to become as we age. We need a heart transplant which only God can perform. And that heart transplant will begin to give us holiness as a consequence of the change of heart.

Holiness has both positive and negative aspects. 1 Corinthians 6:9-11 lists a variety of sins that anger God. Another list is found in Galatians 5:19-21. 1 John 3:15 added the sin of murder, both physically and in its figurative sense of hatred of Christians, to Paul's lists. If one or more of these are presently ingrained in your character, you are not truly a Christian—you are not beginning to resemble Jesus Christ in your character. The passage makes it clear that many Christians at one time were committing such sins habitually, not just by temporary lapse but as an expression of the person's essential character. When Jesus Christ put the new heart within the person, he or she changed from the core of the soul outward. Galatians 5:22-24 has one positive list of the characteristics of a Christian; 1 Corinthians 13 describes love in detail and would complement the Galatians passage. Another list is in 2 Peter 1:5-7. In this life you will never be perfect. Yet it is necessary to be holy to enter heaven, not as a matter of making oneself fit for heaven but as evidence that Jesus Christ has put a new heart in you to prepare you for heaven. Jesus Christ paid the entire price for every Christian's ticket to heaven; holiness is your required boarding pass to go through the gate and enter the airplane.

I am concerned that many of you reject holiness as too confining for you. This was true of Israel in the days of Jeremiah. Like the homeowner, would you rather stay in your current spiritual home and go down in a blaze of glory? Is it so important to have a hot time now that you will court a hot time forever? If you burn now with sinful passions, whether for power, greed, forbidden sex or whatever else may be sinful and refuse to change, God will administer poetic justice and you will burn forever and ever. To indulge your freedom to do anything you want for the moment are you willing to be confined in the Lake of Fire forever?

So many people brush off Christians who sound spiritual warnings like the workers who knocked on the homeowner's door. Others, as in ancient Israel and in the Roman Empire before Constantine, actually kill the messengers. Compounding the offenses by mistreating or killing the messenger did nothing to lessen the spiritual danger. What of you? I can't decide for you, but as an ambassador from a God alien to you I can present His offer: repent of your sins, believe in His Son the Lord Jesus as your Savior and Lord and as equal with His Father, and plead with the Father for the new heart which He will give to all who will ask in honesty for it. Will you repent and receive?

HOLINESS: STANDING WITH GOD EVEN IF IT MEANS STANDING ALONE ON EARTH

Holiness. When I say the word I sound like I'm from an alien planet. If we understand holiness as purity in thought and conduct, practically everyone thinks that any who strives to be holy is a wet blanket. If we go back to the original meaning of holiness, which meant to be set apart, once again we are running against the contemporary current. With our modern cell phones, we seem to dread being set apart from our friends. We have to keep in touch on every little detail. Not only that, but our Internet communications encourage conformity over originality. Even apart from the differences in technology, one has a hard time imagining any of the old prophets who stood practically alone fitting into the idea of constantly asking our peers for their approval or their opinions. Elijah stood alone against 850 government-sponsored prophets on Mt. Carmel. Jeremiah stood against the government in counseling submission to Babylon because God told him so. In an Internet age both would have been "flamed" if not worse. Holiness is one way to stick out from the crowd. One can remember the Japanese saying that "the nail that sticks up gets hammered down." This has been true to some extent in every age, but in the Internet age it has become especially true.

Jesus Christ warns us that *"Wide is the gate and broad is the way that leads to destruction, and there are many who go in that way. But tight is the gate and narrow is the way that leads to life, and there are few who find it."* Matthew 7:13-14. At least in matters of faith and conduct, you cannot have easy conformity to the world's habits and have God's holiness at the same time. And holiness is not an optional "extra" to the Christian life. *"Pursue peace with all, and holiness, without which no man shall see the Lord."* Hebrews 12:14. When we refuse to conform to what is wrong in the world, we need not be uncouth or rude, but we must be firm and even stubborn. We must pursue holiness without hesitation even though the temporary costs may be large.

Here is one place where it is easy to go wrong, to assume that holiness is primarily some forms of outward conduct and the absence of other forms of outward conduct. The outside world will see evidence of holiness in outward conduct, but the root cause of such holiness is not self-discipline. God promised to Israel and by extension to people of all races of humanity: *"I will put My law in their inward parts and write it in their hearts, and will be their God, and they shall be My people."* Jeremiah 31:33. And Ezekiel said, *"A new heart also I will give you and a new spirit will I put within you, and I will take the stony heart out of your flesh, and I will give you a heart of flesh. And I will put My Spirit within you and cause you to walk in My statutes; and you shall keep My judgments and do them.* Ezekiel 36:26-28.

Holiness starts with a new heart and then grows outward as the Holy Spirit goes to work. Thoughts, speech, attitudes, emotions and conduct all begin to change so that the person with the new heart is becoming more like Jesus Christ. In time the change becomes noticeable even to casual acquaintances. Reputations change. To take an extreme example, Saul of Tarsus was once known as a strict Pharisee who maintained a strict separation from all Gentiles and also the fiercest enemy of what came to be called Christianity. Then he became known as a defender of the same faith that he had once sought to destroy (Galatians 1:23), and finally grew to become the primary apostle of Christianity to the Gentiles.

Some of you may want no part of such a change. You may like yourself the way you are. But if you have understanding, you would find nothing to like about your future if you persist in refusing to believe in the Lord Jesus as Son of God and as Savior from sin, including your own. God does not appreciate you calling Him a liar about His Son and further would not appreciate anyone using His Son's holy name as a curse. Suppose that you do not want the holiness that God plants in the inside of the new human heart. Then what do you want? A place in the Lake of Fire forever? That would be anything but cool—in any sense of the word. Do you want to be gulping in "rotten eggs" gas with every breath? Do you want to be throwing up from the dregs of the wrath of God? Do you want to be separated forever from God and from all things good that He has made? Because God is Himself holy, if you refuse to be separated from your sins you end up separated from God Himself in everlasting fire prepared for the Devil and his fallen angels.

Let us look at another historical example. Jeremiah gave the prophetic word that Israel should surrender to God's appointed overlord, the King of Babylon. Most refused and many died as a consequence. A modern example is the American treatment of Japan after World War 2 once it had surrendered. The fighting and the killing stopped. Today God has appointed a much better and kinder overlord for the entire world than the old King of Babylon or even General MacArthur. That ruler is Jesus Christ, the Son of God. He will implant a new heart with the germ of holiness in anyone who will surrender, just as the King of Babylon spared the life of Jeremiah and of any Jew who surrendered to him. This everlasting ruler embodies both love and power and is infinitely greater than any political ruler, past, present or future. You need to surrender to Jesus Christ if you have not already done so. Your war against Jesus to defend your sins is futile and fatal. But if you surrender now you will find Him a loving and compassionate Master, full of grace and truth. His love is forever and yours for Him will be likewise. You may find yourself separated from your current friends, but so what? You have in the Lord Jesus a new friend more fulfilling than all sinful friends put together. And you will have His promise of everlasting joy and foretaste of that joy now even if you should be plunged into a crisis immediately. The everlasting gains are incomparably better than the temporary things you may lose.

HOLINESS IN THE FACE OF OPPOSITION

There is a strong tendency among Christians to compromise their faith when faced with temptation. Yet such compromise is seeking common ground for an agreement when that common ground does not exist. In the course of the search for phantom common ground, a Christian can easily fall into a ditch. If you read the accounts of the Temptation of Christ in Luke 4 and Matthew 4, you will find that there was no common ground between the Lord Jesus Christ and the Devil, even though the Devil quoted Scriptures out of context in an attempt to deceive the Lord Jesus. Instead of negotiating, the Lord Jesus repelled the Devil at every time, using Scriptures accurately quoted and applied. *"What fellowship does righteousness have with unrighteousness? And what communion does light have with darkness? What concord does Christ have with Belial? Or what part does a believer have with an infidel? And what agreement does the Temple of God have with idols?"* 2 Corinthians 6:14-16.

In this present time of social media the urge to get along with our peers becomes very strong. But the world wants Christians to participate in activities that we know are sinful. Consider 1 Peter 4:3-4: *"For the time past in our lives is sufficient for us to have done the will of the Gentiles, when we walked in lasciviousness, lusts, excess of wine, revelry, banquets and abominable idolatries, in which they think it strange that you do not in the same excess of riot, speaking evil of you."* In other words, the world is filled with party animals and it expects and even demands that you behave the same way. Jesus Christ and the Holy Spirit demand the opposite. Speaking specific of worship of idols but using words that speak equally well to party animals, the Apostle Paul delivers the command of the Holy Spirit, *"'Wherefore come out from among them and you be separate, and touch not the unclean, and I will receive you and I will be a Father to you and you shall be My sons and daughters,' says the Lord Almighty."* 2 Corinthians 6:17. So in place of the superficial connections with our peers in the world with no regard for God, God offers us a permanent family relationship that even survives death.

Of course a Christian and an unbeliever can cooperate in secular matters such as jointly repairing a car, constructing a house or maintaining a utility plant. The same laws of physics apply to all people on earth. Christians and non-Christians in the present day can work side by side in the workplace, although the scope for such cooperation is growing narrower with the rising tide of moral evil in our day (November 2013 as I first write this). But in spiritual matters there never can be agreement, and as the Last Days draw closer the conflict will become sharper and sharper.

Our Lord Jesus warns that *"If the salt has lost its savor, with what shall it be salted? It is from then on good for nothing except to be cast out and to be trodden underfoot by men."* Matthew 5:13. While the world may hate a consistent Christian, it will have a sneaking respect for him or her. But the one who under pressure loses his or her Christian distinctiveness will lose all respect. Such people will not get the temporary comfort of being part of the crowd, nor will they receive the respect given to the brave, even by enemies. During the Battle of Leyte Gulf, the Imperial Japanese Navy in 1944 stood in respect to the courage of the American destroyer and destroyer escort crews bobbing in the ocean who had charged battleships and heavy cruisers in the line of duty. As Peter says, *"It is better, if this is the will of God, that you suffer for doing well than for doing evil."* 1 Peter 3:17. Earlier in the same letter, Peter said, *"Having your behavior honest among the Gentiles, that whereas they speak against you as evildoers, they may by good works which they shall see glorify God in the day of visitation."* 1 Peter 2:12. If you are a believer, an important part of winning unbelievers is to maintain your good works and so earn their respect. Without such respect there is little probability that they will listen to what you say. If you are noticeably inconsistent in your Christianity, there is a much higher probability that the world will dump on you because they perceive you as a hypocrite. Accordingly, we are told to *"Watch. Stand fast in the faith. Be strong."* 1 Corinthians 16:13; see also Ephesians 6:10 and 2 Timothy 2:1. Part of being strong is being holy and part of being holy is being strong.

Being strong does not mean being insulting to an opponent or even an enemy. Paul wrote to Timothy to behave like this: *"in meekness instructing those who oppose themselves, if God perhaps would grant them repentance to the acknowledging of the truth."* 2 Timothy 2:25. Our Lord Jesus said to *"Love your enemies. Bless those who curse you. Do good to those who hate you and pray for those who despitefully use you and persecute you."* Matthew 5:44. Moses, an exceptionally meek man, was also patient. And yet Moses gave no ground on issues of fundamental truth. Neither can we. In love for all we must be strong. It's easy to say but hard to do.

HOLINESS: THE DEPTH OF CONVERSION

It has been said that Churchill and Hitler disliked one another instinctively even though they never met. In this case Churchill was right. Some of us have had an experience where we instantly either liked or disliked another, knowing virtually nothing about the person. Clearly these reactions are not rational decisions based on tested and verified information.

Research on the brain is just beginning to discuss the hippocampus, the amygdala and the limbic system, which we now believe are the part of the brain that deal with snap judgments and instinctive reactions. When these portions of the brain are in control, there is no time for the rational part of our brain to stop us from having thoughts which we would be ashamed to expose in public and especially ashamed of before God. This instinctive part of our brain also has sin as do our more rational parts of the brain. Our inability to restrain totally evil thoughts, whether of lust, pride, envy, rage, murder, suicide or other sinful thoughts, is one strong evidence of our helplessness to live a sinless life which would not need the atonement of Jesus Christ. The Apostle Paul teaches at length from personal experience in Romans 7. While it would be far worse to speak (and note James 3:5-8) or act based on such thoughts, the thoughts themselves are sinful and merit everlasting punishment apart from Christ's atonement. For examples, consider Matthew 5:28, James 2:1-4 and James 4:1-7.

Since the final objective of God's salvation is to make us completely perfect citizens of His new heaven and new earth, His salvation involves a change in our sub-conscious brain as well as our surface emotions and reasoning. These are portions of our brain that we essentially can't control, but the Holy Spirit can. So conversion is not confined to our rational selves but includes our instinctive selves as well. Our tastes change. Our measurement of other people will change over time as we get to know God better. Our patience will grow. There will not be perfection on earth but over time one anticipates major change. Conversion does not stop at the surface of a person; in fact it starts on the inside and works its way out as the "engrafted Word" within does its work. James 1:21. Even our sub-conscious is being straightened out much as braces slowly straighten out teeth. Over time the results and rewards are obvious.

HOLINESS: COUNTDOWN

I am about to tell you an imaginary story, something like a parable about the Last Judgment. This story will not take place as related, but its spiritual principles can be found in the Bible. We will see the hopelessness of trying to approach God through self-effort, through achievement or through keeping the commands of the Law. We should start at the Last Judgment, where someone whom I will identify as Saul (perhaps like Saul of Tarsus before his conversion) protests that his sentence to eternal death in the Lake of Fire is unjust. Saul started off with the protest, *"Did I not prophesy in Your Name? Did I not cast out demons in Your Name and do many marvelous works?"* (adopted from Matthew 7:22)

When the Lord Jesus answered with the command, *"Depart from Me, you cursed, into everlasting fire prepared for the Devil and his angels,"* (Matthew 25:41, compare Matthew 7:22) Saul in turn protested that he was good enough to merit heaven or at least an opportunity to prove how good he was for reconsideration for entry into heaven. Of course holy angels could have dragged Saul into the Lake of Fire and confined him there, but the Lord Jesus took this opportunity for an eternal reminder that any human being who enters heaven enters by grace, not inherent merit. So He addressed Saul, "I will give you the chance you seek, but on My terms. I was crucified for 6 hours on a cross when I lived in a mortal tabernacle, like the one in which you lived on earth and unlike the body I have now. My Father accepted this endurance as sufficient to pay for all of the sins of His chosen people from every ethnic origin under heaven. Three of those 6 hours were in total unnatural darkness. For this test I will give back to you your mortal tabernacle which has died in its prime condition when you lived in that tabernacle on earth. But on your part you must agree to be nailed to a cross as I was and endure the 6 hours as I did, including the three hours of unnatural darkness. I will place a countdown clock before you so that you will know how much time is left. However, you cannot sin in thought, word or deed during those 6 hours. Until the very end, you cannot have water nor pain-killers and you will have to endure derision in your native language from those witnessing the test, as I did from the members of the Sanhedrin (Mark 15:29-32). If you are sinning, the countdown clock will run backwards instead its normal forward direction. If you pass this test, I will permit you to enter heaven.

If you fail, you will be punished with utmost severity for all eternity. Do you agree?"

Saul agreed. Then the Lord Jesus gave the necessary commands concerning the retrieval of Saul's mortal human body and the production of a suitable cross and the implements of crucifixion. The countdown clock was produced.

"Saul, are you ready?" "Yes," he replied. Then the Lord Jesus commanded that the crucifixion begin and the angels obeyed instantly. The countdown clock was set to 6 hours.

Saul felt the initial searing pain hit. His heart began to race. His wounds bled. His shoulder muscles cramped. He could hardly catch his breath; he had to apply pressure on his nailed feet in order to give his diaphragm enough room to clear his lungs. Then he heard the grim humor and laughter at his expense. "Hey Saul! What mighty works can you do now?" "If you are worthy of heaven, get off that cross!" Then Saul glanced at the countdown clock and saw that already it was running in reverse, meaning that he would have to suffer even longer. Saul became angry at what he perceived as the unfairness of the test. He was good enough for God! To his horror, this very thought accelerated the reverse action of the countdown clock. Then Saul began to scream and curse and the clock ran backward faster and faster. He wept, but that was no help either. Saul tugged at the nails to no avail except to increase the pain. He wanted to yell at the Lord Jesus but he was now out of breath. Saul was reduced to shaking his head in anger and mouthing curses that he could no longer scream out as he wished. Darkness had not fallen yet, but even being able to see others gave no encouragement to Saul. Their holiness and loyalty to the Lord Jesus separated them from Saul psychologically, so Saul complained about both his pain and his isolation. The clock kept spinning backward like a counter measuring a country's national debt. Finally, after a few minutes, Saul recognized the hopeless of his situation. He endured the pain of getting his breath and screamed out, "It's hopeless. Get me out of here and off this cross!"

But the Lord Jesus answered Saul, "You made your promise and your bargain. I knew it was hopeless from the beginning. On earth you had the entire Law warning you that it is hopeless to approach God by your work or your merit. Your confession comes too late and your judgment has already been pronounced."

Then to the angels the Lord commanded, "Leave Saul as he is and transport him in his present state to his place in the Lake of Fire. He is to stay there forever hanging on his cross, being perpetually crucified. And make sure that Saul is aware at all times of the severe displeasure of his Creator, including the use of belittling sarcasm. Make sure that any sounds he makes cannot reach heaven and disturb the joy of those who through faith abide with Me forever. I need not be disturbed further with him either. Leave a way that anyone in heaven who finds it helpful can observe Saul for a few moments as a reminder of the pain that I endured on My Cross."

Then the Lord Jesus repeated His sentence to Saul, *"Depart from Me, you cursed, into everlasting fire prepared for the Devil and his angels."* The sentence was executed.

The parable is ended, but what are the lessons? One obvious one is that *"All have sinned and come short of the glory of God."* Romans 3:23. Saul and all those like him will receive the wages they have earned: *"The wages of sin are death, but the free gift of God is eternal life through Jesus Christ our Lord."* Romans 6:23. A new chance is not what we need. Rather we need a new heart and a new spirit. *"A new heart also I will give you, and a new spirit will I put within you, and I will take the stony heart out of your flesh and give you a heart of flesh.* Ezekiel 36:26. Then note the consequence of the new heart and the new spirit will be holiness. *"And I will cause you to walk in My statutes, and you shall keep my judgments and do them."* Ezekiel 36:27. First comes the new birth (represented here as a heart-lung replacement) and then comes the start and growth of holiness on which God insists.

A second, closely related lesson is that we cannot approach God with our own achievements. Even our breath and our food is given to us. There is no such thing as a human achievement done without God. *"All our righteousnesses are as filthy rags."* Isaiah 64:6. The evil ones tried to stress what they had done as reported in Matthew 7, provoking further the wrath of God. We can come only on the basis of what Jesus Christ has done in ransoming us from our sins to be God's people. *"The Son of Man did not come to be served but to serve, and to give His life a ransom for many."* Matthew 20:28. By yourself you can never attain heaven and you can never escape hell.

And we cannot forget the awful, perpetual punishment of those who refuse the grace of God. Both Ezekiel 3 and Ezekiel 33 lay upon those who know the grace of God the duty to warn others within their reach of the spiritual danger ahead. We are not responsible for the response of our hearers, whether few or many. We are responsible to sound the warning when God opens the opportunity and to actively seek for such opportunities. In some circles we will be about as welcome as a skunk at a picnic, but what really matters is God's opinion, not human consensus. In reality people will be just as stuck in the Lake of Fire as our imaginary Saul in our parable was stuck to his cross. God demands that we be clear in our warnings and we can do no less.

Saul in the parable eventually confessed the truth of his helplessness under pressure, but it was too late. *Now is the accepted time; behold, now is the day of salvation."* 2 Corinthians 6:2. If there are any who do not trust the Lord Jesus Christ as Lord and Savior, ask Him to put that new heart and new spirit within you without delay. No particular formula is necessary. But do not put this off. *"Do not boast yourself about tomorrow, for you do not know what a day may bring forth."* Proverbs 27:1. I plead with you to call upon Him right now in faith that He will answer.

HOLINESS OR HELL?

A growing number of celebrities and others less well known are now proclaiming their same-sex affinities in the open. The leader of the Duck Dynasty when asked by GQ Magazine quoted the following Scripture from the Holy Bible when asked about this:

> *Don't you know that the unrighteous shall not inherit the kingdom of God? Do not be deceived: neither fornicators, nor idolaters, nor effeminate, nor abusers of themselves with mankind, nor thieves, nor drunkards, nor revilers, nor extortioners shall inherit the kingdom of God. And such were some of you, but you are washed; you are sanctified; you are justified in the name of the Lord Jesus and by the Spirit of our God.* 1 Corinthians 6:9-11.

The network carrying the television show of the Duck Dynasty suspended the head of Duck Dynasty from production for the expression of his faith and then reinstated him under pressure. But what does God think about this?

We have historical examples of societies in which same-sex practices were prevalent. One could start with Sodom and Gomorrah, once prosperous cities near the east side of what is now called the Dead Sea, the lowest elevation on the surface of the earth which is not covered by ocean. When Abraham gave Lot his choice of land in the general vicinity of the Promised Land because their prospering herds were too large to keep together, Lot chose Sodom and its surrounding area because of its prosperity. It is apparent that Lot's wife enjoyed life in Sodom. But Lot and his family soon found trouble. A coalition of kings from the general area of modern Iraq came to enforce an agreement that Sodom and the surrounding area pay tribute when payment was withheld. Lot was taken hostage. But the action of the kings confirms that at this time Sodom was prosperous and was able to pay tribute. The raid was initially successful and would have been well worth it if Abraham had not intervened through the power of God.

So Lot was set free and returned to Sodom and was well enough known to sit at the gate of the city. He was sufficiently wealthy to be able to provide hospitality to strangers. But we should not imagine that Lot enjoyed his riches. As Peter said in 2 Peter 2:6-8:

> *God [the antecedent and grammatical subject in 2:4] . . . turn[ed] the cities of Sodom and Gomorrah into ashes [and] condemned them with an overthrow, making an example to those who thereafter should live ungodly, and delivered just Lot, vexed with the filthy behavior of the wicked (for that righteous man dwelling among them vexed his soul from day to day with their unlawful deeds) . . .*

So Lot was an unhappy man living in a moral cesspool just as Mr. Robertson finds himself in company unpleasant to him now. Material prosperity did not compensate for the division within Lot's family. Lot was isolated among his neighbors as a righteous man living in a culture where "anything goes." Neither Lot's wife nor his prospective sons-in-law followed Lot's lead. When Lot saw the strangers in the city square, he knew that for their protection that he would need to offer shelter. Little did Lot know that their presence would soon be necessary for his protection!

What was God's response? Fire from heaven! Mass destruction! Lot escaped with only his life and his daughters. Even his wife looked back and was made into a pillar of salt. Where Lot's story ends in the Bible, he lived in a cave because his wealth was burned up in Sodom. His daughters got him drunk, probably because they believed that their father was the last person available to give to each one a child. The precise location of Sodom and Gomorrah was unknown for centuries; archeologists now believe that they have uncovered two ancient cities in the devastated area that may have been the destroyed cities. Even today the area is desolate and the Dead Sea will not support ordinary marine life.

Sodom became a byword of a society so immoral that it provoked God to rain judgment on that society. For example, consider Deuteronomy 29:23 and 32:32, Isaiah 1:9-10, 3:9 and 13:19; Jeremiah 23:14, 49:18 and 50:40; Ezekiel 16:48-56; Amos 4:11 and Zephaniah 2:9 in the Old Testament.

The Lord Jesus Christ warned of judgment to come that would be even worse than that which had already been meted out to Sodom and Gomorrah in Matthew 10:15 and 11:23-24, Mark 6:11, and Luke 10:12 and 17:29. Similar usage is also found in Jude 7 and in Revelation 11:8.

Romans 1:20-32, written through the Holy Spirit (note the title "Holy" for the character of the Spirit of God) by the Apostle Paul, is another passage which denounces multiple forms of sin in vigorous language. Within this general passage are verses 26-27, which also bear on Mr. Robertson's response concerning same-sex practices:

> *For this cause [idolatry as mentioned in verse 25] God gave them*
> *up to vile affections, for even their woman changed the natural*
> *use for that which is against nature, and likewise also the men,*
> *leaving the natural use of the woman, burned with their lust one*
> *for another; men working with men that which is unseemly, and*
> *receiving in themselves the recompense of their error which is right*
> (the archaic word "meet" is in the King James version).

To set these verses in their context of the denunciations of various forms of sin, the reader is urged to read all of Romans 1:20-32. I quote them here to focus on the issue raised by Mr. Robertson's critics. God hates all sin and will hate every person who deliberately clings to his or her own sin of whatever type or combination. In truth, Mr. Robertson was relatively mild in his warning compared to the complete words of both the Old and New Testaments on same-sex practices.

God has not changed. He is just as angry at modern sin as He was at the sins of Sodom and of other ancient civilizations which He has overthrown in the past, starting with civilization before the Flood. Revelation indeed prophesies the final destruction of current human civilization in favor of direct dictatorial rule and judgment by Jesus Christ. Only the time is in question; the fact of coming destruction is a dead certainty.

Like the passage in Romans 1, the passage that Mr. Robertson read does not confine itself to same-sex practices nor to sexual sins in general. It is part of a theme in Holy Scripture that those who cling obstinately to unholy conduct of any type will not enter the kingdom of heaven. For other Scriptures of this type, one can read 1 John 3:15 and Revelation 21:8. But Mr. Robertson's passage offers hope for anyone willing to change from their favorite forms of sin, whatever they may be. There is practically no form of sin that has not been forgiven through the blood of the Lord Jesus Christ. As 1 Corinthians 6:11 states, we are "justified" in the name of the Lord Jesus, meaning that we have been declared righteous even though we are not inherently righteous. We have also been "washed" and "sanctified," showing that our moral nature and behavior have changed. We must start to change after having been declared righteous, but all sorts of sin, even the most heinous, can be and has been "blotted out" (Acts 3:19, see also Colossians 2:13-14). Redemption is available to the repentant.

But what of those who refuse to repent and worship the Lord Jesus Christ? They have spurned their only hope. A tragic and horribly painful eternity is their future. Mr. Robertson desires to offer hope, but too many not only turn away from real hope but also slap the hand that offers that hope. Their future will resemble Sodom's past and may well be even worse. In love Christians have a duty to sound a warning as Mr. Robertson has done. His hearers have a duty to God to heed his warning and to repent of their sins. In love we pray that many will do so.

HOLINESS: APPROVAL, DISCIPLINE, OR BOTH?

There is constant debate over the place of approval and discipline in raising children and in pastoring a church. Some pastors will avoid preaching against specific sins in order to avoid offending some in the audience, whether a church member or not. Other people can be so vitriolic against a particular sin that they leave people with no hope. I observed one parent in court who simply could not acknowledge that anything her child was doing was wrong. Her method was to be positive no matter what. According to other testimony, the child had issues of concentration and self-control and would get out of her seat when this was not permitted. At the other extreme, I have also observed at least one set of parents who would almost never praise a child. Nothing that the child could do seemed to satisfy them. Does either of these approaches help bring holiness?

Let us consider how God as Father deals with His children. With salvation He puts His stamp of approval on us. *"So far as the east is from the west, so far He has removed our transgressions from us."* Psalm 103:12. *"You also as living stones, are built up a spiritual house, a holy priesthood to offer up spiritual sacrifices, acceptable to God by Jesus Christ."* 1 Peter 2:5. *"Let us draw near with a pure heart with the full assurance of faith . . ."* Hebrews 10:22. And yet He disciplines us, sometimes severely. *"Every branch [in Me] that bears fruit He purges, that it may bring forth more fruit."* John 15:2. The word "purges" is a strong word, from which we get our word catharsis. And even more strongly we read in Hebrews 12:6-8, *"For whom the Lord loves He chastens, and scourges every son whom He receives. If you endure chastening, God deals with you as with sons, for what son is there whom his father does not chasten?"* The word "scourge" in Hebrews 12:6 is the same word used for what the soldiers did to the Lord Jesus the night before He was crucified, so real rigor and pain is involved, but for good purposes instead of the evil meant by the soldiers. God is not like the hateful parent of Proverbs 13:24 who does not care whether his or her children do right or wrong and therefore does not bother to correct them, even by corporal punishment for severe or dangerous wrong. God is a loving Father Who corrects when necessary. So as parent and pastor we will have to act both in approval and in discipline. In both cases love is the motive behind the action. Love may be best expressed at various times by acceptance, discipline or a mix of both.

Within our own souls we must both rejoice in God's acceptance and respond to His correction. We need the "full assurance of faith" and at the same time cultivate the fruits of the Spirit. Self-control is one example of that fruit (Galatians 5:23). So holiness is a combination of acceptance and discipline rather than either one alone.

HOLINESS & ANGER

Only God is capable of purely righteous anger with no sin mixed in. As James says, *"The wrath of man does not work the righteousness of God."* James 1:20. And Paul warns that we cannot permit our anger to simmer in Ephesians 4:26-27: *"Be angry and do not sin; do not let the sun go down on your wrath, neither give room to the Devil."* Anger is an excellent alarm bell that something needs attention. But if we ignore the alarm bell and let it keep ringing, it will drive us crazy. That "something that needs attention" may be within ourselves or may involve another person or an external situation, or some combination. Anger is not sinful of itself; anger is one of the characteristics of God. *"God is angry with the wicked every day."* Psalm 7:11. Yet despite His anger God *"sends His sun to rise on the good and on the evil, and His rain on the just and on the unjust."* Matthew 5:45. As Romans 9:22 says, *"What if God, willing to show His wrath and to make His power known, endured with much longsuffering the vessels of wrath fitted for destruction . . ."* So God does not immediately unleash His anger, and we cannot let anger take control of us either. There will be times that God will guide us to forgive the offender and leave any corrective or punitive action to Him. Proverbs 19:11 says, *"The discretion of a man defers his anger, and it is his glory to pass over a transgression."* The day will come when God does unleash His anger in full and takes His vengeance, but for the moment I write concerning the time before He does so.

If the Bible calls for corrective action, anger is a good motivator to get us started on the needed corrections. If we have good reason to be angry with ourselves, we cannot stop there and let our anger run riot; we need to repent and to correct the source of this anger rather than berate ourselves perpetually. Or suppose one of your children has punched another without cause. Of course you will be angry. That anger may propel you to take appropriate disciplinary action—possibly a spanking or other consequences or a combination of consequences designed to correct the child and warn him or her not to repeat the offending behavior. But you cannot let that anger control you to the point where you yourself lose your temper and perhaps punch the child in retaliation for his blow. There must be self-control to keep your actions within the bounds of Holy Scripture and short of any risk of inflicting injury. Your words and tone of voice must likewise remain controlled for correction, not for cursing or denigrating the offender.

We should also remember that a man who gets angry easily is not yet ready to serve as an elder or deacon in the church. Titus 1:7 (elder) and 1 Timothy 3:3 (extended to deacons in the word "likewise" in 1 Timothy 3:8).

Cain was angry with God for not accepting his offering. But Cain could not reach God to retaliate. So Cain instead murdered Abel, who was within reach. This is a Biblical example of uncontrolled anger vented on an innocent person who did not cause the problem in the first place. Much child abuse occurs this way also. The safest way to vent anger is in prayer to God, Who is able to handle emotions that we human beings cannot. Physical exercise will help. So will reading the Scriptures to let the first heat of the anger pass. The Scriptures will also guide us as to what corrective words or actions might be appropriate. For most people, letting their anger control them will cause them to over-react and probably cause further damage in the process. I am not saying to ignore anger, but I do plead that all of us would plead for the Holy Spirit to control and direct our anger, recognizing our own sinfulness in the process.

BENEFITS OF HOLINESS WHILE WE
AWAIT HEAVEN

In the previous studies we have touched on the necessity of holiness as evidence of the new birth in Jesus Christ. Now we should look at the benefits of holiness to a Christian while he or she is waiting to be ushered by angels into the presence of Jesus Christ forever. Let's start with worry. Our Lord Jesus counseled us all against worry during the Sermon on the Mount (Matthew 6:25-34). So many people suffer from diseases of stress. We know that stress can aggravate heart and cardiovascular disease, ulcers and many other illnesses. Road rage can kill. I will not promise you that all Christians will be healthy, but I can say that many qualities of holiness ordinarily do have a property of supporting physical and emotional health. For example, the Lord Jesus said the night before His physical death to His disciples, *"Peace I leave with you; My peace I give to you—not as the world gives I give to you. Let not your heart be troubled, neither let it be afraid."* John 14:27. This peace will reduce stress that otherwise would be intolerable. Just imagine having that peace when facing crucifixion. And consider how Peter was able to sleep in his cell the night before he was supposed to die. The angel had to wake him up. Acts 12:7.

Patience is another holy virtue that helps a person bear hard times. Job is legendary for his patience under trial. Just imagine having 10 funerals for your children who have just died in a mass disaster. And then imagine having boils all over the body so that there is no comfortable posture even to lie down, with all of the consequent pain and fever. Job was nearly an outcast. His wife in Job 2:9 advised him to "get it over with"—to curse God and die. Job had a terrible odor because of his disease. And Job's three friends misjudged the situation on the erroneous theory that Job's misfortune proved of itself that God was angry with Job over his monumental sin. In some passages they were extremely harsh. At times God does rain down judgments on a grievous sinner as punishment for his or her sin (see David's confession in Psalm 38 and again in Psalm 51, and look at the threats at Jezebel in Revelation 2:22-23 for but two of many examples in Scripture) but this was not true in Job's case. But Job endured and never denied his faith in the one true God. His health was restored, he was given 10 more children and he was given an exceptionally happy old age before death. He also had his prayer answered concerning the resurrection, that his words would be recorded forever. (See Job 19:23-29) This is an eternal monument to Job's faith under trial, since it is recorded in Holy Scripture that shall not fade away. Patience is practical for dealing with hard times and hard people.

Holiness makes a person more attractive to God. As Ephesians 5:22-33 teaches, whether we are married or not on earth we are engaged to be part of the Bride to be married hereafter, as described in Revelation 19. We know something of the lengths to which brides on earth go to prepare themselves for their ceremony on earth. It is not unusual in the USA for brides' families to spend $20,000 or more on their weddings. As important as a human wedding may be, it is far more important to prepare for the Marriage Supper of Jesus Christ. How can this be done? Consider the teaching of Peter: *"Whose adorning let it not be the outward of plaiting the hair, or the wearing of gold, or the putting on of [elaborate] clothing, but let it be of the inner person of the heart, of a meek and quiet spirit, which is in the sight of God of great price."* 1 Peter 3:3-4. Even on earth, I certainly would much rather marry the right person in a simple ceremony with a simple reception than marry a contentious person with a ceremony and reception of great cost. For confirmation, see Proverbs 21:9, 21:19, 25:24 and 27:15-16.

If we truly love the Lord Jesus, we will express our love for Him by obeying Him. *"If you love Me, keep My commandments."* John 14:15. *"Jesus answered and said to him, 'If a man loves Me, he will keep My word, and My Father will love him; and We will come and make Our abode with him.'"* John 14:23. Once again in John 15:10 the Lord Jesus said, *"If you keep My commandments, you will abide in My love, just as I have kept My Father's commandments and abide in His love."* As a human bride stirs her man's love by looking at him, so we as part of His Bride should stir His love. In turn we will receive love also. One example is Hebrews 12:2, which reads in part, *"Looking to Jesus, the Author and Finisher of faith . . ."* This verse is normally read concerning endurance, and properly so. But it can also be read in the context of our love for Him.

To analogize a woman's jewelry to preparing for the heavenly marriage, consider the fruit of the Spirit starting in Galatians 5:22. Love, as the supreme jewel in all of Christianity, is mentioned first and foremost. *"He that loves another has fulfilled the Law . . . Love works no ill to his neighbor; therefore love is the fulfilling of the Law."* Romans 13:8, 10. Galatians 5:14 agrees. Then come joy, peace, patience, gentleness, goodness, faith, meekness and temperance. A woman whose spirit is arrayed with these will be beautiful with or without jewelry made on earth. Since every Christian on earth is preparing to be part of the Bride of Christ, each of us should be looking into the "mirror of the law of liberty" (taken from James 1:23-25) to see if these jewels are properly polished and are in place, and whether they are becoming. If we see something amiss in a physical mirror, we fix it. Even men notice a spot where the shaver missed and go back over it. It is far more important for us to correct ourselves when we see something amiss spiritually. In so doing we are behaving like a bride-to-be who is especially careful about her appearance—and I would hope being even more careful about the state of her soul and of her love for the Bridegroom. Every day there is some form of preparation for that great and glorious marriage supper of the Lamb in Revelation 19.

Titus 2:14 explains our holiness as one of the primary purposes for which our Lord Jesus submitted Himself to crucifixion: *"Who gave Himself for us, that He might redeem us from all iniquity and purify to Himself a special people, zealous of good works."* We have not been redeemed to do as we please but as He pleases. It is His pleasure and our good also that we be holy and from that have and display the fruits of the Spirit. Joy and peace are two examples of how holiness benefits us in the end even though it means abstaining from harmful things that give a short rush of pleasure (often followed by a crash of despair). In contrast to the short pleasure of sin, joy and peace last for eternity and are infinitely more valuable. Self-denial is a necessary part of holiness, just as exercise is a necessary part of physical fitness. Both are good for us and contribute to our beauty when we finally become part of the Bride at the Marriage Supper of the Lamb of God, Who gave Himself for us. So let us live as if we are rehearsing for that last great marriage, because that is indeed true. There is a saying that is true both in music and in athletics—you play the way you practice. Let us concentrate as we rehearse for heaven. Let us prepare in holiness for our ultimate place in the close presence of Jesus Christ our Lord.

HOLINESS & HUMILITY GO TOGETHER LIKE VANILLA ICE CREAM AND CHOCOLATE SAUCE

If you have a desire to be holy, you will have to be humble. Even the very beginning of salvation involves a certain beginning of humility. Nicodemus, an experienced teacher, was told by the Lord Jesus that in spiritual terms he had to start over like a baby. *"You must be born from above."* John 3:7. (I am using the literal Greek here instead of the more familiar English phrase "born again.") Saul of Tarsus was awestruck when he saw the risen Lord Jesus on the Damascus Road. Note the humility in Saul's very first question to his Lord: *"What will You have me to do?"* Acts 9:6. Although David may have been further along, note the humility in his reaction to God making a covenant with him: *"Who am I, O Lord God? And what is my house, that You have brought me so far?"* 2 Samuel 7:18. Even more strongly did Job humble himself after he had heard God: *"I abhor myself and repent in dust and ashes."* Job 42:6. Most of all, as the Son of Man the Lord Jesus *"humbled Himself and became obedient to death, even the death of the cross."* Philippians 2:8. If the core of holiness is the imitation of the Lord Jesus Christ, then we must imitate Him in His humility. In Philippians 2:5 we are exhorted to *"Let this mind be in you that was also in Christ Jesus."* And we should remember that on the last night of His earthly life the Lord Jesus did the work normally done by a slave in washing the feet of His disciples.

Obviously humility and pride as opposites should not co-exist, although we know that because we are yet imperfect that some pride may remain in us as an impurity which must be progressively removed. If humility is praised, we should expect pride to be denounced, as indeed it is. In James 4:6 we read that *"God resists the proud but gives grace to the humble."* As Solomon instructed, *"Pride goes before destruction, and a haughty spirit before a fall."* Proverbs 16:18. *"A man's pride shall bring him low, but honor shall uphold the humble in spirit."* Proverbs 29:23.

We should not think of humility as weakness. Here again the Lord Jesus is the supreme example. I would challenge you to read honestly the Sermon on the Mount (Matthew 5-7) in one sitting. Imagine yourself being one of the crowd and hearing each word distinctly. Then ask you how much weakness you perceive. Especially consider that at the finish of Matthew 7 that the Lord Jesus compared his sayings to a strong rock that can bear the entire foundation weight of the house, even in a great storm. My wife and I once owned a house in Frederick County, Virginia that was literally built upon a rock in about 1940. From what I could see in the basement and in the old land records, it appeared that the builders could not remove a tremendous boulder from the basement and therefore left it in place and built on top of it. The foundation in two places rested on that boulder. This was a physical illustration of our Lord's last illustration in the Sermon on the Mount. The Lord Jesus, though humble, claimed that His sermon could support the weight of an entire life, and then He proved it for the rest of His time in a human body.

Returning to Proverbs 29:23, we should see that humility, honor (at least with God) and holiness all go together. Very often people who are most honored with God are dishonored by the majority of humanity. If we are dishonored by people for the sake of Jesus Christ and of His holiness, then everything we may lose on earth will be restored in heaven. Job is an example here, having had 10 children to replace the ones whom Satan had killed and having been blessed with twice the wealth that he lost. Even David, who lost 4 children because of his sin with Bath-sheba, also had 4 children born to him through Bath-sheba according to 1 Chronicles 3:5. Our Lord Jesus gives a yet more expansive promise, *"And everyone who has forsaken houses, or brothers, or sisters, or father, or mother, or wife, or children, or lands, for My name's sake, shall receive one hundredfold and inherit everlasting life."* Matthew 19:29. Let us abandon human pride and embrace honor with God, humility and holiness.

HOLINESS: THE EXAMPLE OF DAVID'S LIFE (PART 1)

Jesse's wife woke him up in the small hours before dawn and told him that her time was coming yet again. Having had seven previous sons, she knew the signs well. They had wondered whether the seven sons that God had already given them was their limit, but God had given Jesse and his wife one last child a few years after the seventh. In their Bethlehem tent, Jesse got fresh bedding and did what he could to ease his wife's pain. She gripped his arm, strong from his work with crops and livestock, against her pain as the contractions increased. Just before dawn her eighth child appeared. He was a healthy boy with a strong cry and a ruddy complexion. Even now in the dark he showed vigor as his mother offered her breast. His parents named him David.

David was born into a troubled nation. He was of the tribe of Judah, one of the largest tribes of Israel. He had a Moabite great-grandmother Ruth, wife of the famous farmer Boaz. Among the tribes of Israel there were loose ties. Only recently had Saul of Benjamin been anointed by Samuel the priest as King over the twelve tribes, and his hold was still tenuous. Saul has started under pressure from Nahash of Ammon in the east and from the Philistines in the west. The Philistines had a local iron monopoly which meant that the armies of Israel were inferior in their weaponry when fighting against them. Some years before the Israelites had lost possession of the Ark of the Covenant to the Philistines. Many Israelites gloomily concluded that God had abandoned them, not thinking that God had indeed abandoned them partially and temporarily because of their lack of loyalty to God, the sovereign over Israel and indeed over the entire earth. Some in Israel worshiped idols in direct violation of the Ten Commandments. The lessons of men such as Gideon, not to mention Moses, Joshua and Caleb, had been largely forgotten. Bethlehem was not adjacent to any border of Israel and so was not in as much danger of invasion as border districts, but the tribes surrounding Israel were coalescing into national states that in some cases were experimenting with aggression.

Israel was at a low ebb spiritually. Samuel, the prophet and priest, was truly a great man, but his own sons were corrupt. The tribal elders could

91

see that Samuel's children were unsuitable as leaders, so they wanted a king just like the nations that were forming around them. In so doing, they were rejecting God as King (1 Samuel 8:7). God had His reasons for instructing Samuel to grant their request even though it was wrong, but the nation's trust was in men—in many cases in a single sinful man—rather than in God. In David's infancy, Saul reflected this attitude in doing what he thought was best rather than following the counsel of God or even of God's representative Samuel. As David grew, Saul's tendencies to depend on his own wisdom grew worse.

Earlier, Israel had had a great individual champion fighter and judge named Samson who had helped keep the Philistines in check despite their iron technological superiority. He was now dead, having taken a good deal of the cream of Philistine society with him. Without God's help, the Israelites were no match for the Philistines in flat terrain in man-to-man combat. The Israelites were with God's help capable of defeating the Philistines in the hills or by ambush, so the Philistine conquest of Israel was never complete. But now Samson was dead and the Philistines were about to acquire their own rising young strongman named Goliath. At David's birth, he probably was not quite ready for military service, but his size must have set him apart even as a very young child. (He grew to be over 2 feet taller than Kareem Abdul-Jabbar, whose height was already strikingly apparent as a first grader in New York.)

At least the former great powers Egypt and Babylon were in eclipse, giving time for smaller peoples such as Israel to take root in the territories that God had allotted them. The same was true of the other nations surrounding Israel. Egypt through the centuries had never fully recovered from the loss of its army as it tried to pursue the people of Israel through the Red Sea. Assyria, later to be centered in Nineveh, was yet over 2 centuries in the future. So the time around David's birth in the providence of God was a time in which there was no great power dominating what we now call the Middle East.

It might help if we proceed clockwise from the southwest to understand who bordered Israel at this era. One could start in the far southwest with Egypt, who was not a major factor. Closer in were the Philistines on the Mediterranean seacoast on the southwest and west. These worshiped a fish-god and still looked to the sea for many of their cultural memories. To the northwest of Israel were the Phoenicians, the people of Tyre and Sidon. Later this was to be a source of great evil, but that is over 2 centuries down the road from the time we are now considering. This is roughly the modern Lebanon; as ruler David was able later to form an enduring alliance which secured his northwest boundary. In the northeast were various small city-states that had not yet consolidated into something like modern Syria. David sought alliances in this direction too. To the east with the kingdoms of the children of Lot: Ammon and Moab. These were related to Israel but as a rule did not share faith in the God of Israel. To the southeast was Edom, also related through Abraham but not sharing faith in the God of Israel. A raiding people, the Amalekites, wandered to the south of Israel. They were hereditary enemies of Israel. From them had come the false prophet Balaam, who had taught Balak to seduce Israel spiritually and morally because he could not prevail by direct force. The enmity persisted to David's time and beyond.

As David grew, his first assignment of significance was guarding the family sheep. This is the type of thankless job that the youngest children inherit from their elder brothers. Yet we shall see that God used this to prepare David for his life's work. And it was this work that David was doing when Samuel had anointed David privately to the King of Israel in Saul's place.

Ancient shepherds had to be independent. Often the sheep were too far away for a cry of "Wolf!" to be heard by the adults in the area. So David was often on his own. Like many kids, he practiced throwing and similar athletic pursuits. In his case instead of throwing a "Spaldeen" or similar rubber ball, David would have been using a slingshot. But both his distance and his accuracy improved steadily as he practiced. One would imagine that he progressed from aiming at a tree to aiming at a particular branch and then to a still smaller target.

If David had not already been taught this, he would have learned that smooth stones were the most accurate. Modern rifling to impart a spiral would not have been available to David. For the same reason as a baseball pitcher wants seams in a baseball to make it break, David wanted to avoid seams or similar irregularities because he needed to throw hard and straight. So David learned to use smooth stones as his ammunition. 1 Samuel 17:40 reflects accurate science; if David had to use his slingshot in an emergency, the last thing he needed was to throw a knuckleball.

In fact at least twice David faced emergencies in which his slingshot was necessary. On one occasion a lion attacked his flock and on another the predator was a bear. In both cases David rescued the lamb from the predator, as much later the Good Shepherd would rescue His sheep from the Evil One, the Devil. Psalm 23 reflects David's experience as a shepherd. David did not attribute his survival, or the survival of the sheep in his care, to his own skill. David gave glory to God for his escapes (1 Samuel 17:34-37). But we should observe that David did use rudimentary science to good effect.

Although David did not know it, God was preparing David for his first great crisis, his battle with Goliath. This started innocuously with David carrying food supplies to his older brothers fighting with King Saul against the Philistines. As he delivered the supplies, David heard the scuttlebutt about the giant Goliath and especially heard how Goliath defied the God of Israel. Then David heard Goliath for himself. This made David indignant and aroused his fighting spirit. David had faith that God would strike down someone who trashed His name and seemed surprised that nobody had challenged Goliath yet. He was ready to be the one.

King Saul and the rest of the army of Israel were looking at Goliath's size and strength, while David concentrated on God's strength. David had a totally different view of the situation based on faith while the others used only human eyesight. As one reads the account in 1 Samuel 17:22-58, it is plain that David meant what he said—that God would enable him to destroy Goliath. David staked his whole life on it. Even at this young age, that's faith!

God's previous preparation of David as a shepherd came into play. David had no intention of coming into range of Goliath's sword or even of his spear. Instead, David used a vary ancient form of artillery—the slingshot—to stay out of Goliath's range. Compared to a lion or a bear, the massive Goliath was a slow and relatively easy target to hit. As with the wild animals, the strike had to be accurate to the head to stop the attack. The Biblical text is not completely clear, but it seems as if the stone knocked Goliath unconscious rather than killing him outright. David needed a heavier weapon to finish Goliath off, so he seized Goliath's own sword and cut off his head. With this the triumph of Israel, and above all the triumph of the God of Israel, was complete and obvious.

Now David became entitled to the rewards that King Saul had promised to the man that would challenge and kill Goliath, starting with Saul's daughter Michal as his wife. But David probably was not fully ready for marriage and needed more seasoning in any case before he could grow into the place of leadership that God had chosen for him. This is one of the reasons why Saul was not overthrown immediately when God first rejected Saul (1 Samuel 16:1). God propped Saul up while He was seasoning David to become King of Israel in fact as well as by Samuel's anointing. As Saul began to comprehend the trend, he became more and more jealous of David to the extent of attempted murder. David, though already anointed as King, began a long ordeal of being chased by Saul which prepared him to rule well when power finally flowed into his hands.

HOLINESS—THE EXAMPLE OF DAVID'S LIFE (PART 2)

We now move forward in David's life to his early middle age when he seemed to be at the height of his powers. Some of this material has been discussed before. A refresher should be helpful, especially because we will this time concentrate more on the consequences of sin and less on the grace of God that comes through notwithstanding the sin.

To help understand why holiness is so necessary in the life of every Christian, let us learn from David the far-reaching consequences of a major lapse in holiness. David was coming off twin peaks of spiritual achievement: (1) The retrieval of the Ark of the Covenant from the Philistines and its eventual transport to Mount Moriah, which became part of Jerusalem and the site of the Temple; and (2) The granting of mercy to Mephibosheth even those he was of royal lineage from the rival house of Saul, the rival king who had sought David's death. Earlier, David had captured Jerusalem from the Jebusites, one of the Canaanite remnants left over from the time of Joshua. David was being used of God to write Psalms, which became portions of Holy Scripture. Even more, David had become a party to a covenant with God in which He promised to provide in perpetuity a descendent to rule over Israel. (See 2 Samuel 7.) It is fair to say that in this portion of his life David was on a roll.

The first domino of sin did not even originate in Israel, but rather in Ammon, a neighbor of Israel. King Nahash of Ammon had died. So far as I can tell from Scripture, we first encounter this Nahash when he attacked Israel very early in Saul's reign (1 Samuel 11—I assume that there were not two kings of the same name but rather one king with a long reign). Having been beaten off in that encounter, he learned a lesson and appears to have kept the peace with Israel thereafter. Now roughly 50 years later King Nahash was dead, as we read in 2 Samuel 10:1-2. Since Nahash in his later years had kept the peace with King David, David sent a delegation to express Israel's condolences and to offer continued friendship with Nahash's son and successor. In modern times the United States often sends its Vice-President as the leader of a delegation to attend the funeral of a deceased foreign leader. But Nahash's successor was a smart-aleck and humiliated the Israeli diplomats by forcibly cutting their clothes and shaving half their beards and then sending them away. Angered by this diplomatic insult, David ordered an invasion of Ammon. But for an unknown reason David did not go with his army as he normally did. This did leave David in a position to view temptation and then to succumb.

Instead of being with his army, David was on the roof of his palace, which in all likelihood was built on one of the highest hills in Jerusalem. With this vantage point David could see out over the city, and he saw Bath-sheba bathing on her roof, which should normally have been private. Her husband, Uriah, was one of the leading soldiers in David's army, which would explain why their home was close to David's palace and within his range of vision at the very peak of the hill. At the sight of Bath-sheba David's holiness crumbled into lust. The downward spiral was rapid. David had a tryst with her and Bath-sheba became pregnant. David then called Uriah home so that he would go to his house and make love to his wife; David's purpose was to provide an explanation for Bath-sheba's pregnancy which did not involve his encounter. But Uriah, in solidarity with his soldiers, refused to enter his house. So David sent Uriah back to the front bearing sealed orders that Uriah be left to die at the hands of the enemy. When Uriah did die, David took Bath-sheba into his palace. But God was not fooled and He refused to ignore David's grave lapse from holy living.

Now the dominoes continued to fall in David's life as God sent Nathan the prophet to deal with David. Nathan first told a parable to force David to face his sin and then warned David that from now on his family would be rocked by conflict, which came true for the rest of David's life.

DOMINO #1: David's son conceived with Bath-sheba while Uriah was alive died seven days after birth;

DOMINO #2: David's son Amnon lusted after his half-sister Tamar and with the help of a clever cousin devised a cover story that lured Tamar into a position where Amnon could and did rape her. David was extremely angry but took no action, probably remembering his own guilt;

DOMINO #3: David's son Absalom, a full brother to Tamar, about 2 years later invited Amnon to a party and had Amnon ambushed and killed in revenge for the rape. Absalom then fled to the land where his mother had been a princess before she married David;

DOMINO #4: Joab, David's army commander, brokers the end of Absalom's exile. Absalom alleges inattention to the administration of justice by his father. I suspect that there was some substance of this in the aftermath of David's guilt, but Absalom's real purpose was to build support to overthrow his father and take the throne for himself. Absalom did try and for 90 days David had to flee Jerusalem for the outskirts of northeast Israel. In the ensuing battle, Joab personally kills the rebel Absalom despite David's orders to the contrary.

DOMINO #5: In David's old age near the end of his reign, David's son Adonijah arranged for his own coronation without David's approval. David's wife Bath-sheba and his high priest both urged David to act, and he himself had Solomon coronated as his successor and heir to the throne. Adonijah backed down for the moment but sought David's last companion as his wife after David's death. Solomon for that reason had Adonijah executed as a threat to an orderly and undisputed succession. This completed the sequence of four un-natural deaths among David's children.

We just went through a thumbnail version of the most obvious consequences of David's sin involving Bath-sheba. A more careful examination is warranted.

One observation is that the Devil can strike from an unexpected direction to tempt us to sin. In this case the first step in the chain reaction was the unwarranted discourtesy of the new King of Ammon to David's ambassadors. Understandably, this angered David. But even when anger is justified, it can easily put us off our spiritual guard. The Bible gives me no information as to why David did not leave with his army for the invasion. That looks like such an innocent circumstance, and yet it put David in position to receive serious temptation in the form of seeing Bath-sheba bathing on her rooftop. And David fell for it.

When considering the far-reaching consequences of sin, one should note that David's forces conquered the Ammonites and put the surviving men in their armed forces to forced labor. The entire country was occupied for many years. The consequences to the people of Ammon for the folly of their new king throwing away the friendship of Israel were dire. There is one more appearance in the Bible in alliance with Moab and Edom against King Jehoshaphat of Judah, but the nation never again attained significant power and was swept away by Babylonia. Digressing down this thread, we do not see a revival of either Moab or Ammon after the fall of Babylon as we do of Israel. The inheritance of the children of Lot eventually fell to the children of Ishmael, the Arabs. It is reasonable to think that this smart-aleck king started the final downfall of his own country.

Returning to David, we should see that David at first only wanted to cover up his sin—he did not start out to become a murderer. But when Uriah refused to sleep in his house, David resorted to murder to conceal his previous sin. Also, David's primary concern was to conceal his sin from his countrymen. Apparently he had forgotten about God for the time being. We dare not do that.

God did not ignore David's sin even though David himself did his best to ignore it. Psalms 38, 51 and 32 are the primary psalms that center on David's life shortly after his great sin. They make it clear that David felt miserable in general and that David had lost his normal masculine ability to enjoy sexual intercourse with a wife (Psalm 32:4). He described persistent fever—perhaps dengue fever, also known as "breakbone fever" (Psalm 51:8 may be a reference to this especially painful fever.). David probably spent most of the 9 months of Bath-sheba's pregnancy under one form or another of physical weakness, not to mention the emotional stress.

When the first child was born to Bath-sheba, God found it necessary to strike that child dead to make clear in a public manner His displeasure with David. Not even fasting was enough to induce God to relent. Bath-sheba no doubt suffered terribly losing this child, but David knew that it was primarily his responsibility. So David consoled Bath-sheba as best he could amidst his own grief.

Another consequence of David's sin was an apparent reluctance to administer justice. After all, David was a murderer himself, although a forgiven murderer. It would be a natural reaction for David to shy away from justice as a man conscious of his own guilt. So Absalom exploited this gap not from any passion for justice but as a wedge issue to turn the loyalty of the people away from his father David to himself. See 2 Samuel 15:2-6. Then Absalom went to David's old capital of Hebron and had himself declared king, meaning full-scale civil war within Israel. For the moment Absalom's power was rising and David was in danger of being killed by his own son. But God ordained and arranged the reverse—that Absalom delayed his attack on David and then was hung up in a tree by his own long hair (much as some paratroopers were hung up in trees by their parachutes) and was killed by Joab, David's army commander and the same man who had brokered Absalom's return from exile. Joab had created a monster, and now he extirpated that same monster that he had helped create.

David's reluctance to administer justice even extended to the rebel Absalom. He had ordered that Absalom not be harmed, but Joab disobeyed. In this case disobedience was right; there would be no peace in the kingdom while the rebel Absalom remained alive. Solomon came to the same conclusion years later about Adonijah. One of the many reasons that we must avoid sin is to keep ourselves sufficiently pure that we can rebuke and correct sin in others, taking precautions lest we ourselves be tempted (Galatians 6:1). This is especially necessary for heads of families and for elders in the church. David was scarred in this part of his life for years by his sins against God involving Uriah and Bath-sheba.

Years later David was confronted with Adonijah arranging for his own coronation without David's approval. Although David was now old and both Bath-sheba and the prophet Nathan (who had confronted David over Bath-sheba years before) had to rouse David, David did take sufficient action to safeguard Solomon's succession to the throne to the exclusion of Adonijah, as is related in 1 Kings 1. David's final advice to King Solomon is recorded in 1 Kings 2, centering first on obedience to the Law of God and then on two potential sources of rebellion in the kingdom: Shimei and Joab. Solomon quickly identified Adonijah as a third rebel. In due time Solomon caused the execution of all three, including David's son Adonijah. This was the fourth son of David that died an unnatural death, after the first baby with Bath-sheba, Amnon, Absalom and finally Adonijah. We do not know what ultimately happened to Tamar. One would guess that she lived in seclusion, but the Scripture does not give us definite information. Certainly Nathan's warning to David about continued trouble in his family came true, and all because of one sequence of sin starting with lust for Bath-sheba and ending with the murder of her husband Uriah.

But with the disasters came touches of mercy also. David lost 4 sons, but 1 Chronicles 3:5 tells us that David had four sons through Bath-sheba. Solomon had a very close relationship with Bath-sheba. Adonijah tried to exploit this (1 Kings 2:13-17). Her instruction (Proverbs 1:8) as well as that of David helped prepare him to instruct the whole world through the Holy Spirit in Proverbs, Ecclesiastes and Song of Solomon. Both human genealogies of the Lord Jesus run through Bath-sheba and David. So we need to see both the mercy of God and the terrible consequences that a lack of holiness can cause.

HOLINESS MEANS BEING PEOPLE OF THE HOLY SCRIPTURES

"Blessed are the pure in heart, for they shall see God." Matthew
5:8. *"The words of the Lord are pure words, as silver tried in a
furnace of earth, purified seven times."* Psalm 12:6.

Moral and spiritual purity are closely related to being set apart to God, to
holiness. If we are to have these qualities, our thoughts, words, silences,
motives and actions or abstentions from action must line up with God's
holy words. The Bible is the ultimate standard by which our internal
thoughts, feelings and emotions and our external conduct will be judged.
As a beginning we must make ourselves aware of what the Bible says as
far as we are capable. Especially in America, ignorance of the Bible is
no excuse when so many versions of the Bible are offered for purchase
cheaply. People in countries where Christianity is discouraged or even
illegal under human law take great risks to get some form of the Bible
because they know how important it is and how much of a blessing it
is. We have no excuse if we fail to make room for the Bible in our busy
lives. Even blind people can and do get either a Braille version or a spoken
version to feed their minds and souls. As David sang, *"Your word have I
hidden in my heart, that I might not sin against You."* Psalm 119:11.

When the Lord Jesus summarized the Law into its compressed essence,
He used one verb, *"love."* This is the sacrificial form of love. Psalm 119 is
an extended form of David's love for the words of God. This corresponds
to *"You shall love the Lord your God with all your heart, with all your soul
and with all your mind."* (Matthew 22:37-Luke 10:27 adds "strength" to
the three in Matthew) Since the Lord Jesus sacrificed His human body
for us to save us forever, it is only reasonable that we sacrifice ourselves for
Him. Gratitude demands that much even though our sacrifice will never
come even close to His. This is a working compass for holiness—denying
and sacrificing ourselves for Him. How that works out in practice varies
enormously from person to person.

As to the branch of the summary of the Law, *"You shall love your neighbor
as yourself,"* (originally in Leviticus 19:18 and quoted in Matthew 22:39

and referenced in Luke 10:27), 1 Corinthians 13 gives an extended picture of this. As we come closer to meeting these particular Scriptures, we will come closer to God's holiness. The Ten Commandments give a summary of what to avoid in loving God and in loving our neighbor, and many other Scriptures give more specific guidance for both the emotions and for the mind. But the basic principle of love gives us an overview into which we can fit the more specific commands and warnings of Scripture. In some respects we are working on two jigsaw puzzles to get an accurate picture of holiness: (1) The life of Jesus Christ and secondarily the lives of the best servants of God, and (2) The Law of God, with love as the straight pieces along the edge of the puzzle from which we can start. In this life we can never expect to finish either puzzle, but we can make progress and learn. To do this we must become and remain people of the Bible, in thought, speech and action. Sometimes there will be costs of various kinds on earth. Showing love cost the Good Samaritan money. Telling the truth eventually cost Isaiah his physical life.

I was just reading Marcus Rainsford's exposition of our Lord's prayer as High Priest in John 17 when a title caught my eye. Part of the prayer of the Lord Jesus in John 17:17 to His Father was, *"Sanctify them through Your truth; Your Word is truth."* The Bible is a primary means of our holiness, and our holiness is so important that the Lord Jesus personally prayed to His Father for it while still on earth. He still intercedes for us now (Romans 8:34). The Lord Jesus' prayer will be answered. For our own good, we should joyfully join in the prayer of our Savior and regularly read and meditate on His Word with the intent of become more holy and more like our Lord Jesus.

Holiness does not mean that we become static while on earth. To the contrary, we must grow and bear fruit of holiness. John 15 makes it clear that the Father prunes His children like grapevines to increase their fruitfulness. Romans 6:22 ties the two together: *"Having been set free from sin, you have your fruit to holiness, and the end everlasting life."* And Hebrews 12:10 gives the purpose of God's discipline: *". . . that we might partake of His holiness."* While progress is not always even and there will be setbacks from time to time as there were with Peter and Barnabas (Galatians 2:11-13), the overall trend will be progress in grace and holiness. Have confidence—faith—as Paul did: *"Being confident of this very thing, that He Who has begun a good work in you will continue it until the day of Jesus Christ."* Philippians 1:6. At the end of the day, your sin will be destroyed, Satan will be destroyed, but you will share in the everlasting triumph of Jesus Christ.

HOLINESS OF THOUGHT AND SPEECH

The Third Commandment addresses prohibited speech: *"You shall not take the name of the Lord your God in vain."* The "name of the Lord" includes not only of God the Father but of the Son and of the Spirit as well. Cursing the name of Jesus Christ and using His name as a curse are equally within the sweep of this prohibition. Why do we hear the names of Jesus Christ and of His Father said as a curse more than any other? Because the human conscience has some dim awareness of their sovereignty and the sinful human heart insists on expressing its rebellion against the sovereignty of God notwithstanding the warnings of conscience.

When we examine the Sermon on the Mount and its treatment of the Commandment against adultery, we see that the Lord Jesus prohibited not only the act but also the inward desire that leads to the act (Matthew 5:27-28). Applying that principle to the Third Commandment, its prohibition reaches not only to the words but also to the thoughts behind the words. That impatient half-expressed or suppressed curse when something goes wrong is also a root of outward sin and is itself sinful. These thoughts get formed before our rational mind can even weigh them. Scientists are just beginning to learn about the limbic system and the amygdala. Control of the rational mind is absolutely necessary but it is not sufficient to exterminate all sin from us. If we are to be purely holy, our first emotional and instinctive reactions would have to be perfect just as our Father in heaven is perfect.

Let me try an analogy to restate this. We know from nature that the land will spring up with weeds if left untended. When we weed, to do a perfect job we not only have to cut down the foliage but also kill the weed to its very roots. For example, to kill a dandelion or a thistle we have to pluck out all of its roots. Nothing less will prevent a recurrence. It is not only the noxious plants that are the problem. It is also that the land itself has been cursed (Genesis 3:17-19). The ultimate solution will be a new heavens and a new earth (2 Peter 3:13, Revelation 21:1).

Following the analogy, we have already been given a new heart and a new spirit (for example, see Ezekiel 36:26 and 2 Corinthians 5:17), but these have been implanted into an old body which remains mortal and sinful. Romans 7 is a major Scripture teaching this. We also retain for now sinful impulses side-by-side with the indwelling Holy Spirit (see Romans 8). By analogy with the new earth which would reject weeds were any to attempt to take root, we are awaiting a new body and a completely purified heart and spirit that will have no sinful impulses whatsoever, which would reject temptation instinctively were any temptation to be presented. The Lord Jesus in His earthly body was able to do this even in the face of the Devil himself.

My first reaction is somewhat like that of Isaiah as described in Isaiah 6: I am undone because I am a man of unclean thoughts. Damnation is what I deserve at strict justice. This gives me a new sense of just how wide the gap remains between the absolute holiness of the Lord Jesus and the rudimentary holiness that the Spirit so far has worked within me. My second reaction is thanksgiving, inadequate though it is. I should be giving thanks to the Holy Spirit for putting up with my unclean thoughts as He indwells me. Instead of the coal off the altar, I have been given the Holy Spirit within me to start purifying the moral sewer that remains from my unsaved nature (Ephesians 1:13-14). The Spirit has been working patiently on this for many years. I should be giving thanks to the Lord Jesus for living an absolutely righteous life that is put to my account so that I can be saved and God's justice will still be satisfied. I should be giving thanks that the blood of Christ has blotted out the Law itself as it would apply to my case (Colossians 2:14). I should be giving thanks that all of my sins, from the smallest to the most vile, are legally and permanently separated from me as far as the east is from the west (Psalm 103:12). What is more, they shall be separated from me by experience as well. None of this could I do myself. Having been dead spiritually (Ephesians 2:1-2), I could not even make a contribution to starting this process. Now, having been made alive by no power of my own, I can labor to a very limited extent to become more holy and less offensive to God by nature, but I could never even approach this on my own. And even that life—that saving faith—is a gift from God and did not originate within me (Ephesians 2:8-10).

Tertullian, a very early church theologian, is widely believed to have said that he was made for nothing but repentance. Allowing for literary exaggeration, there is truth in what he said. But I would suggest a blend of repentance and thanksgiving instead of repentance alone. I think this would get us closer to the Biblical target. I include thanksgiving because it brings joy, a necessary component of the Christian life. It is not easy to imagine how a focus totally on repentance will allow for much joy; a focus on repentance only looks at our sin (indeed necessary!) but little on our deliverance from sin through Jesus Christ. I think that we need both in a proportion that I cannot quantify with any precision. That proportion may fluctuate during our lives. So as an oversimplified formula just to get started on fellowship with God, let me suggest a combination of repentance and thanksgiving to start our sharing person-to-person with Almighty God through Jesus Christ. Humility should be included as well.

BENEFITS OF A HOLY REPUTATION IN HEAVEN

We have spoken of holiness as important preparation for meeting the Lord. There is another purpose for holiness—that of receiving rewards from God for faithfulness. As you look through the seven letters from the Lord Jesus to the seven churches in Revelation 2 & 3, you will see rewards offered to those who are faithful and overcome various forms of evil. We can offer these rewards back to the Lord Jesus during our heavenly worship as the 24 elders kept taking off their crowns as they worshiped Him in Revelation 4. These rewards are ours, and yet they are His because He died for us, bought us completely and redeemed us and all that we have for Himself. And one will see that these rewards, although undeserved, are based on holiness in one form or another.

Consider Proverbs 10:7: *"The memory of the just is blessed, but the name of the wicked shall rot."* This makes a tremendous difference in eternity because we know that the righteous and the wicked alike can feel and communicate intelligently after death. Our Lord Jesus affirmed this directly in Luke 16:19-31. He also said that *"Abraham rejoiced to see My day; he saw and was glad."* John 8:56. When the Lord Jesus walked the earth and spoke these words, Abraham was dead physically almost 2000 years. But Abraham was aware of the prophets who had come after him and knew about the Lord Jesus' life on earth. Moses and Elijah were able to appear on the Mount of Transfiguration long after their physical departures. (Matthew 17:3) There was a resurrection of Old Testament saints on the same day as the Lord Jesus rose from the dead (Matthew 27:52-53).

So intelligence and consciousness persist after the death of this body. Reputation will matter in the afterlife. Hitler is a prime example of a man whose reputation still rots to this day and will rot forever. When I did my thesis on an attempted Communist revolution in Indonesia in 1965, I was dealing with a country which did not exist during the times of the Nazis and which was on the other side of the world. Yet the people instantly understood the anti-Communist pun "GESTAPU" based on the Nazi Gestapo. Indonesia is on the other side of the world, and yet the Gestapo and Hitler were universally hated. So it will be in heaven, and Hitler will know it and suffer forever for it.

One need not be a Hitler to have a foul reputation for eternity. Nelson Rockefeller, former Governor of New York and Vice-President of the United States and one of the wealthiest men in the world, was caught literally with his pants down committing adultery with a younger woman when God summoned him from earth to eternity. In sports, we have in September 2013 seen the importance of last appearances in the cases of Mariano Rivera and Andy Pettitte. Nelson Rockefeller will be remembered through eternity as a man who spent his last energy violating God's commandment against adultery. From what we can tell, there was no repentance, with the consequence (if in fact there was no repentance and faith, something only Jesus can judge) that Nelson Rockefeller will never be permitted to forget his signature last sin and that God Almighty will continuously punish him for it as well as his other sins. One's eternal reputation with God is far more important than most people think.

As a contrast, consider the woman who poured out the fragrant ointment on the Lord Jesus shortly before His death in Matthew 26:13 (also Mark 14:9). The Lord Jesus promised the woman that what she had done would be a memorial for her. Of course it is preserved in the Bible itself. Being recorded in the Bible, her holy deed is remembered in heaven forever, like Job's faith in the resurrection of the dead in the midst of his terrible sickness. His prayer has been answered: *"O that my words were now written! O that they were printed in a book! That they were engraved with an iron pen and lead in the rock forever!"* Job 19:23-24. In the following verses Job states his faith that he would see God with his own eyes notwithstanding his physical death. The Holy Spirit through James tells us *"You have heard of the patience of Job."* James 5:11. In contrast to Hitler, Job and the woman who anointed the Lord Jesus for His burial will be remembered and honored forever for good.

How do you want to be judged by Jesus Christ at the Last Judgment? How do you want to be remembered in heaven? As a holy and loyal servant of the Lord Jesus, or as an evil henchman of the Devil? If you have any sense, you will see that holiness is worth the trouble. As we have said before, holiness is not possible unless and until the Lord Jesus replaces your hard, sclerotic heart with a new softened heart through the new birth. So you must start there, asking the Lord Jesus in faith to save you from your sins. Then the process of holiness begins. Then as Job 14:17 says, *"My transgression is sealed up in a bag, and You sew up my iniquity."* Or as Psalm 103:12 says, *"So far as the east is from the west, so far has He removed our transgressions from us."* The legal forgiveness of sins is the start, and holiness the continuation, of the process by which we will eventually be made fit to enter the awesome presence of God in heaven. As a beginning, we have access through prayer to the Holy of Holies while we remain physically on earth. But then we progress to being present with Jesus Christ at the Last Judgment and finally into all the joys of heaven with Him forever.

HOLINESS & HOPE

Much of the time we think of holiness as difficult, as indeed it is. *"For narrow is the gate and difficult is the way that leads to life, and there are few who find it."* Matthew 7:14. But there is one benefit of holiness that alone is worth all the trouble: the sure hope of victory over death for every believer. Death kills our current temporary body but catapults our souls into the very presence of God Himself. Why then should we be afraid of death? The Apostle Paul was not: *"For me to live is Christ and to die is gain."* Philippians 1:21. Paul reaffirms that it is better to depart to Jesus Christ in Philippians 1:23. Holiness will enable us to look death in the eye in the sure expectation of eternal victory. Quoting from Isaiah, Paul in 1 Corinthians 15:54-57:

> *So when the corruptible shall have put on incorruption, and this mortal shall have put on immortality, then shall be brought to pass the saying that is written, "Death is swallowed up in victory." O death, where is your victory? O grave, where is your sting? The sting of death is sin, and the strength of sin is the Law. But thanks be to God Who gives us the victory through our Lord Jesus Christ.*

Even to a Gentile ruler who did not know the Lord Jesus Christ, Paul was able to avow his willingness to face death if he had committed a capital offense. Acts 25:11. One of the roots of Paul's courage was his knowledge of the true nature of death for a Christian as a transition from earth to heaven and from incomplete holiness to complete, total and permanent holiness and fellowship with Jesus Christ and with His Father in heaven. Paul was not afraid to die. So Paul persevered despite all of the physical hardships summarized in 2 Corinthians 11:20-28. And that list was not the complete list for all of Paul's life, because Paul's wild ride ending in shipwreck at Malta had not occurred yet when 2 Corinthians was written. Truly the Lord Jesus spoke prophecy to Ananias when He instructed Ananias to baptize Paul: *"For I will show him how great things he must suffer for My Name's sake."* Acts 9:16.

When one reads the list of physical hardships in 2 Corinthians 11, it is easy to see why God gave Paul the gift of living as a single man instead of as a married one. The sheer amount of travel would have worn out even a legendary Amazon. Imagine as a wife watching your husband being stoned, beaten with rods or being whipped with 39 lashes or surviving at least 4 shipwrecks total. To try a modern analogy, that alone would be like surviving 4 major automobile accidents with totaled cars. Paul is a glorious example of holiness, but his particular holiness is unique among fallen men and his ability to live a holy life as a single adult man is rare. We can learn immensely from Paul and his example, but we must be careful how far we try to imitate his life. For most Christian men, the details of our calling will differ.

The very fearlessness of Paul that made him such a courageous apostle also exposed him to danger. On several occasions God used other brothers to restrain with prudence Paul's willingness to face any danger in any circumstances. In Acts 17:10, the church in Thessalonica sent Paul and Silas to Berea to get them away from a mob. Then in Berea the mob from Thessalonica caught up with Paul, and the Berean believers in their turn whisked Paul out of danger (Acts 17:14). This succession of narrow escapes was hard on Paul as it would be on anyone. When he reached Corinth, the Lord Jesus reassured Paul that he would not be harmed in Corinth and that He had many people to save there (Acts 18:9-10). When Paul later went to Ephesus, God's work through Paul was so powerful that it was squeezing the business of the makers of idols (Acts 19:21-27), who called a city meeting to silence Paul and Christianity generally. Paul wanted to go voluntarily to the meeting, but the other believers prevented him from doing so (Acts 19:30). Their prudence was in this case wiser than Paul's courage.

One can make the same case about Paul's insistence upon going to Jerusalem personally despite warnings from several sources that he would be arrested there. (See Acts 20:22-23, and Acts 21:11-14. In this connection also consider Paul's testimony just after his arrest in Acts 22:18-21.) Whether Paul was right or wrong to persist in the face of warnings to press on to Jerusalem, God's purposes were accomplished. Paul testified in Jerusalem and in Caesarea to both Jews and to petty kings under the Emperor of the Gospel of Jesus Christ, fulfilling the prophecy of Acts 9:15. Ultimately he probably testified to the Emperor Nero as well.

Paul was fearless in confronting sin within the Body of Christ as he was in confronting it in the world. In Galatians 2:4-5 Paul recounts how he spoke against legalism within the Church. In Galatians 2:11-18 (and possibly further) he recounts a confrontation in which Paul rebuked Peter for his inconsistency about treating Gentile believers identically with Jews. Even Paul's missionary partner Barnabas had to be set straight. Later, as recorded in Acts 15:37-39, Paul and Barnabas parted from one another over whether to bring Mark with them on the second missionary journey. Paul traveled with Silas instead. In this case both Paul and Barnabas seemed to have portions of truth. Mark probably was not ready for intense and dangerous missionary work at that time, although Paul near his death when in prison acknowledged that Mark had become profitable (2 Timothy 4:11).

Barnabas took Mark back to his native Cyprus. From church history and what we believe is a reference to Mark in 1 Peter 5:13 (although since Peter was a married man, an alternative possibility is that Peter had his own biological son named Mark) we believe that Mark presented mostly Peter's view of the Lord Jesus in his Gospel of Mark. So Mark's greatest work was most probably not his missionary travel but rather his writing. Paul did not believe that they had time at that point in missionary labor to try to train Mark and was willing to part with Barnabas over the issue. I attribute this to Paul's realization that on-the-job training was impossible under the conditions that they would face; my view is that criticizing Paul for impatience seems plausible but is unfair as one looks at the conditions of missionary labor shown in Acts 16-20.

Even when Paul was absent, he fought against sin vigorously when he learned about it. Both 1 and 2 Corinthians testify to this. In 1 Corinthians 3 he challenged his readers to grow up. I am among those persuaded that Paul wrote Hebrews; we see a very similar passage in Hebrews 5:11-14. In 1 Corinthians 5 he challenged his hearers to banish gross sin from the church by excommunication. After repenting, the man was readmitted as described in 2 Corinthians 2. In 1 Corinthians 6 he warned vigorously about the necessity of holiness for heaven (not as a means to reach heaven but as evidence of genuine conversion, of newness of life). In 1 Corinthians 11 he rebuked them severely for abuse of the Lord's table. In 1 Corinthians 14 he instructed on the necessity for order in church worship. In 2 Corinthians 12:18-21 Paul summarized his previous warnings about the consequences of a lack of holiness and continued his warning in the next chapter. In 2 Corinthians 13:5 he challenged his hearers to examine themselves to verify their salvation. This sounds very much like how we would examine our own bodies for the first signs of physical disease before it has spread. So without question Paul was a champion of holiness within the Christian Church.

So was Peter. After his encounter with Paul over compromise with legalists, Peter did acknowledge that Paul was a "beloved brother" (2 Peter 3:15) and that his letters were Holy Scripture. Peter amplified his warning about the necessity of holiness in the light of the coming destruction of this universe: *"Since all these things shall be dissolved, what manner of people should you be in all holy behavior and godliness, looking for and speeding toward the day of God in which the heavens being on fire shall be dissolved and the elements shall melt with fervent heat?"* 2 Peter 3:11-12

Paul and Peter knew vastly more of the fellowship of the sufferings of our Lord Jesus (Philippians 3:10) than I know or that I am likely to know before He in His mercy takes me to Himself. But apart from the Lord Jesus Himself every saint has flaws as well as strengths from which we can and should learn. Paul himself said that *"we know in part and we prophesy in part."* 1 Corinthians 13:9. If that was true of the great Apostles Paul and Peter, how much more is it true of all of us, including me? As an intermediate goal we can seek to imitate those aspects of their lives that meet our own individual callings from God, but the ultimate example is Jesus Christ Himself. It is part of holiness and of holy humility to recognize that in this life we will not reach our goal on earth. *"[I have not] already attained, nor am I already perfect, but I pursue so that I may eagerly grasp that for which I was apprehended by the Lord Jesus. Brethren, I do not count myself to have grasped it, but one thing [I do]. Forgetting those things which are behind and stretching forth to those things which are ahead, I press toward the mark of the prize of the high calling of God in Christ Jesus."* Philippians 3:12-14. In verse 15 Paul makes it clear that he does not run the race alone. Let us join him even though our pace may be slower. *"Let us therefore, as many as be mature, be likeminded . . . And if in anything you be otherwise minded, God shall reveal even this to you."*

One of the hallmarks of the historical accounts of Christian martyrdoms is the courage with which the martyrs faced death. This is a phenomenon that crosses international boundaries and cultures and eras of time. Stephen (Acts 6 & 7) is the very first martyr. *Foxe's Book of Martyrs* collects accounts from the 1st to the 19th centuries. There are amazing stories of Christian courage in the 20th century as well, and the 21st century is already getting started with its instances of courageous martyrdoms. I cannot measure the total number of the martyrs, but the sum must be huge (Revelation 6:11). It may be that in our particular cases that holiness will involve imitating their courage and facing down death with the sure hope of either resurrection or rapture for fellowship forever with Jesus Christ. If not, we still have that same sure hope of rapture or resurrection to everlasting fellowship with Jesus Christ as a hallmark of holiness.

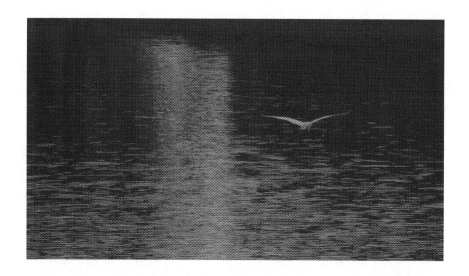

RESURRECTION FREEDOM: AN ILLUSTRATION FROM NATURE

We normally associate flight with freedom. In the Scriptures, a dove frequently symbolizes the Holy Spirit. As Paul wrote in Romans 8:2, *"For the law of the Spirit of life in Christ Jesus has made me free from the law of sin and death."* Because salvation brings freedom to the soul, Paul told even slaves that they were free in Christ even while they were compelled by man-made law to serve their masters (1 Corinthians 7:22). Not even prison can take away the kind of freedom of which Paul wrote. Paul himself knew this from his own times in confinement (for example, 2 Timothy 2:9, which is from but one of several letters in the Bible written in confinement). While that freedom of soul does forbid us certain harmful temporary pleasures, it opens the door to joys that far outweigh the temporary pleasures which God forbids from His great love for us for our own good. Moses understood. He *"esteemed the reproaches of Christ greater riches than the treasures of Egypt."* Hebrews 11:26. And Moses was raised as a prince by Pharaoh's daughter, so he knew the extent of Egypt's riches. Roman exile on Patmos, a prison island somewhat like Alcatraz without the prison buildings, was powerless to interfere with the Lord Jesus giving the Book of Revelation to John.

This flying bird over the pond is an illustration of the work of God through Jesus Christ as stated by Paul in Colossians 1:13: *"[Who] has delivered us from the power of darkness and has translated us into the kingdom of His own dear Son." "If the Son shall make you free, you shall be free indeed."* John 8:36. The resurrection of the righteous to everlasting life in Jesus Christ will be the ultimate freedom, involving freedom from both sin and death.